Be___ ___
it or not

John Lambert

DestinWorld
publishing

Copyright © 2015 John Lambert

First Edition 2015
Published by Destinworld Publishing Ltd.
www.destinworld.com

British Library Cataloguing-in-Publication Data
A catalogue record for this book is available from the British Library.

ISBN 978 0 9930950 7 8

All rights reserved. No part of this book may be reproduced or transmitted in any form or by any means, electronic or mechanical, including photo-copying, scanning, recording or by any information storage and retrieval system, without permission from the Publisher in writing.

In this book, except where otherwise stated, all the Biblical quotations are taken from THE HOLY BIBLE, NEW INTERNATIONAL VERSION®, NIV® Copyright © 1973, 1978, 1984, 2011 by Biblica, Inc.® Used by permission. All rights reserved worldwide.

Dedication

Thanks to all those who interacted with the original blog or the Facebook post they appeared under. Thanks to all who have influenced me in shaping my faith; especially for Sister Anna McDonagh who was the midwife at my spiritual rebirth, Ian and Lynda King who helped to steer me straight especially in the early years, Kathie who has been a wonderful traveling companion in the journey of faith and our four children Anna, Nathan, Joseph and Benjamin who we are delighted to have seen joining us on that journey, each in turn.

Contents

Introduction 7

PART 1: Because it's true

Chapter 1: Out of Nothing 17
Chapter 2: Across the Universe 23
Chapter 3: No Place Like Home 30
Chapter 4: That's Life 37
Chapter 5: Soul to Soul 48
Chapter 6: Good and Bad 57
Chapter 7: What's Wrong? 63
Chapter 8: Beauty from Ugly Things 71
Chapter 9: Don't Go There 81
Chapter 10: With the Benefit of Foresight 87
Chapter 11: The One and Only 95
Chapter 12: Now You're Talking 103
Chapter 13: The Crux of the Matter 111
Chapter 14: Rise and Shine 120
Chapter 15: The Invisible Editor 132
Chapter 16: The Words that Won't Go Away 140

PART 2: Because It Works

Chapter 17: It Does What It Says On The Tin 151
Chapter 18: Looking The Last Enemy In The Eye 162
Chapter 19: When The Sleeping Giant Stirs 171
Chapter 20: No Place Like Home 180
Chapter 21: Like Heaven On Earth 188
Chapter 22: But Deliver Us From Evil 197
Chapter 23: Something Creepy Going On 206
Chapter 24: The Great Unknown 214
Chapter 25: Much Ado About Nothing 222
Chapter 26: Imagine No Religion 234

Footnote 245
Notes 249

BELIEVE IT OR NOT
Introduction

Towards the end of 2012 I was reading an article online about the interrelation between faith in God and scientific knowledge on a particular issue. It was an interesting enough piece. I didn't agree with all of it but I appreciated that the journalist did a decent job of representing different shades of opinion. Let's say it was fair. I saw that the article was open to comments so my curiosity got the better of me and I decided to read on. Oh dear.

The litany of patronising, insulting and often ill-informed comments was just wearisome to read. And not only from the majority of contributors who were vocally antagonistic towards God. The discussion also excited some grammatically challenged interest from some honorary representatives from the Flat Earth Society and the League of Angry Fundamentalists as well. There was descent into caricature from both sides. It was Richard Dawkins meets the leader of Westboro Baptist Church. In short, a troll's playground.

This was not a one-off though. It seems that every time I scroll through the *Have Your Say* or *Comment is Free* section on any Christianity-related BBC or Guardian web posting, whether it be about a new space probe or the Archbishop of Canterbury taking on payday lenders, I seem to find the same angry tones and shocking prejudices. New York City based church leader Tim Keller recently summed up well the increasingly strident intolerance of Christian faith in civic society: "What we are being told is that you are beyond the pale, not just that we're wrong, but that respect for us is wrong... it's not just that you're going to disagree with us, but basically you are saying we really don't even have a right to be in the public square."[1]

The duplication of certain insults (I keep coming across flying spaghetti monsters, sky fairies and imaginary friends) shows that there is a herd phenomenon in which people are taking to throwing someone else's rocks. It makes me sad. I know that some people are ready to say vicious or belittling things only from the safety of anonymity but many do so quite transparently too. It sometimes feels like certain corners of our culture reserve their deepest loathing and greatest ridicule for people like me who believe in the existence of God and the uniqueness of Christ, and who sometimes want to express or commend those views. There are so many poisonous ideologies in our world. At the same time, I see so much good done in society in the name of

INTRODUCTION

Christ. I understand of course that not everyone is going to agree with Christians about a whole range of issues, but it's the strength of feeling, the message board spite, the anger, and the outrage against Christian belief that bewilders me.

Anyway it made me stop and think. Why do I believe in God? Specifically, why am I a Christian? What if Christianity is like *The Truman Show* – an organised fantasy in which I am an oblivious victim? What if the force for good I see and the spiritual feelings I have are just a clever mirage? What if I *do* only follow the Bible's teaching because I am a weak person who is too lazy to think for himself? What if I am just clinging to an infantile myth about eternal life because I am scared of death or something? What if I, like a compliant child being good for Santa, simply never really grew up?

Such questions don't add up to a crisis of faith for me; more a reality check on the soul. This is how we refine thought in our culture. We state something, we test it with enquiry and we arrive at something properly thought through. 'Thesis - antithesis - synthesis.'

I decided it might be a useful exercise to jot down the reasons why I have found Christianity to be believable, to be true. I came up with 26. I then tried to arrange the different reasons in some kind of order. Here's what I came up with:

Firstly, I thought about the origins of the universe, its incredible fine tuning, the improbably life-favouring properties of our planet and the appearance of life from non-living matter. Each gives me some encouragement that my working hunch about the existence of a creator might just be correct. These reasons make up chapters 1-4.

Then there are things to do with the human condition and why there is so much unhappiness and suffering in the world. Philosophers and theologians like Augustine and Aquinas and Luther and Pascal have mused about these things for centuries. What people like them have said helps me to appreciate the reasonableness and coherence of the Judeo-Christian world view. These reasons are explored in chapters 5-9.

The heart of the book is about Jesus. For some, he was an enigmatic and non-violent mystic who said some quotable things; a cross between Mahatma Gandhi and Abraham Lincoln. For others, he was one of many visionary revolutionaries who pushed his luck too far and ended up in an early grave; a hybrid of John Lennon and Che Guevara maybe. There are many other ideas out there about who he was. Chapters 10-14 explore why I think he is totally in a class of his own, deserving of not just admiration but devotion as well.

Chapters 15-17 explain why the Bible gives shape to Christian faith. I know some people hate the Bible, many find it boring and others even reject it as immoral and repugnant. Some of it puzzles me and, honestly, parts of it disturb me. But most of it challenges me and shapes me. I treasure it above every other book. The Bible's remarkable unity, its unparalleled resilience and its amazing potency are among the reasons I believe in its divine inspiration.

Chapters 18-23, explore other ideas, some of which I have gleaned from personal experience. These are not just things I've mused about. They are mostly things I or others have personally seen and felt.

And in the final three chapters, 24-26, I try to explain why I came to reject the three biggest alternatives to being a Christian in today's world (being an agnostic, an atheist or belonging to some other religion).

In Part 1, which makes up the first 16 chapters, I talk about why I believe Christianity *is true*. Part 2 shows some of the ways that Christianity *works*. I am very aware that most people in the Postmodern era don't care if it's true or not. As has been said, most people will only start to become interested in Christianity if they think it might help them have better sex. Otherwise, forget it.

Typically we're told, outside the Church, people don't know much about Christianity, don't care to find out, have little or no religious vocabulary, are more interested in spirituality than religion, relate better to dialogue and conversation than presentation, favour experience over knowledge and prefer visual not textual communication.

Frankly that makes this book a non-starter for a lot of people, I know that. Maybe I'll write another book someday looking at questions like 'who am I?', 'how can I be happy?', 'what happens after I die?', 'why is there suffering in the world?', 'what is the spiritual realm?', 'how does the spiritual realm impact my life?' and 'what is God like?' And maybe even 'how can I have better sex?' That might be a first for a Church of England vicar…

There are some things I say, particularly in Part 2, which touch on this kind of theme but finding answers to these questions were not why I became a Christian.

There are of course counterarguments that you can find for each of the 26 ideas and they're not that hard to find if you want to investigate. A quick search on the Internet will take you where you want to go. I've looked at the alternatives and some are quite thought-provoking. Many seem partly right to me.

It occurred to me that probably none of my 26 ideas on its own would absolutely convince me that Christianity must be true. But together they build a case which satisfies my curious mind and makes sense of my felt spiritual experience. Each chapter is like a piece of a jigsaw puzzle; it's only when it's put together that you can see the full picture and appreciate how all the pieces interlock with the others.

This book first appeared in a series of blog posts, one every two weeks, throughout 2013. Several people encouraged me to publish the series in book form which I was reluctant to do for three reasons. Firstly, what's the point? If you can access the content for free online why pay for a printed version? Secondly, the blog carried important hyperlinks to books, articles, and videos which due to the length of the URLs would be cumbersome and unworkable in written form. Thirdly, there are many, many books on all this sort of thing available from people more learned and eloquent than I am. In what I imagine to be a saturated (and pretty small) market, I imagined I would labour in vain to find anyone interested in publishing it.

But some of my friends insisted that a physical book in the hand reaches some parts that new media cannot reach. And extended footnotes or supplementary chapters can do the work that web links do. And self-publishing avoids sending dozens of manuscripts to publishers who take one look at the title and file a wad of A4 in the wastepaper bin.

I've had to adapt the content slightly for book format and I have made many minor revisions to the original posts. I hope you enjoy what you read. If you are basically sympathetic from the start I hope it will help you see that the faith you instinctively feel has much to commend it. No, you're not strange. It really does make sense and hold together.

And if, as seems unlikely, you read this having decided already that faith is the preserve of village idiots and dangerous sociopaths I hope you will find evidence here that, despite what you may read on social media, Christians do not believe in fairies and unicorns or denounce as infidels those who do. Well, not many of us anyway.

PART 1

Because it's true

Chapter 1

OUT OF NOTHING

It can be proved that 2+2=4, that our home planet is basically blue, and that I am genetically related to my children. However, I do not believe anyone - even I myself - can categorically *prove* that I really love my wife Kathie. But I know I do. Nor can I empirically attest that a Van Gogh masterpiece has any artistic merit - though I feel sure it has.

In the same way, I do not think anyone can prove -or disprove- that God exists. It's not that sort of knowing. Believing in God is more like thinking that a couple must truly love each other if they are still holding hands and making each other laugh after decades of marriage. In fact, they might not love each other at all. They might stick pins in effigies of each other when no one's looking. Appearances can be deceptive. When it comes to establishing the truth of a matter, you have to investigate without prejudice and weigh the evidence of what you observe.

Sadly, I think that this is what so many people don't do. I find that many people, believers and sceptics alike, tend to behave tribally, defending their clan whether it's plainly right or obviously wrong and attacking the opposition even when they clearly have a point. Like an exchange in the British Parliament's House of Commons, debate about God usually generates more heat than light and descends to a competition in who can trade the choicest insults instead of actually considering the matter in hand.

Anyway, here is the first of 26 reasons I think God exists and Christianity is true: **I think that the origins of our universe (indeed, the very fact that there was a beginning to our universe) suggest the work of an originator - a Creator.** "In the beginning..."

Oxford Professor of Mathematics Dr. John Lennox writes about his aunt baking a birthday cake.[2] Though, he says, you can analyse the ingredients and quantify the temperature they must have been heated to in order to deliver the end product, you can't prove that John's aunt made it, or for what occasion, just by examining its properties. All you do know for sure is that it is *there*. And the fact that it is there at all points inescapably to the existence of a baker.

As the age-old philosophical conundrum puts it, why is there something rather than nothing? My first reason for being a Christian is that the universe is there at all and that it came into existence from *nothing*.

If everything that happens has a cause, what caused the creation of the elements, trillions of spinning planets, our beautiful world, vast burning stars, mighty galaxies that are light years wide in span, dark matter, mass, light and energy? And from *nothing*?

Rationalist scientists like Fred Hoyle and humanist philosophers like Bertrand Russell in the early 20th century, no doubt driven by their atheist presuppositions (or perhaps just unconsciously adopting Aristotle's worldview) denied our cosmos had a beginning, arguing that it was just always there. According to this view, there is no need for a creator at all because everything always existed. This was the standard orthodoxy for sceptics for years.

But in 1929 all that changed. The astronomer Edwin Hubble's observation of red shift when studying the light from far away galaxies pointed conclusively[3] to something virtually nobody had ever imagined; *the universe is expanding*. First proposed by Belgian Catholic priest and cosmologist Georges Lemaitre, Hubble confirmed the theory beyond doubt.

By calculating the rate of expansion, cosmologists and mathematicians were then able to work back and establish that the origins of our universe date to about 13.75 billion years ago. The Big Bang. No longer was anyone saying that the universe just always existed. Hubble showed that it *must have had a beginning*. This cosmological model is now virtually undisputed by scholars. It is about as factually certain as the assertion that the Earth is round and circles the Sun once a year.

Lemaitre and Hubble established that the universe had a starting point and cosmologists since then have agreed that the raw materials for everything that exists were... nothing. They just appeared, by themselves, *ex-nihilo*. As if by magic...

Everything that exists -trillions upon trillions of stars and planets spinning in perfectly regular patterns in trillions upon trillions of vast galactic systems- is sourced from the raw materials that came to be on that explosive first day.

I think that this scientific consensus not only fails to rule out, in itself, a wise and powerful eternal creator, it practically calls out for one. Of course, all this *could* have all just happened by itself; the ultimate case of spontaneous combustion. But how? Why would all existing matter; an unimaginable mass of stuff and mind-boggling levels of energy just appear in an instant, without cause, from nothing at all, on its own?

Like the arrival in your driveway of an elegant limousine that had neither designer, nor manufacturer, and now has no driver and no fuel, it just doesn't seem plausible.

As we will see in the next chapter, the physics of gravity and density necessary for the universe to exist at all without collapsing back or emptying out to nothingness have to be incredibly precise. Stephen Hawking and others have attempted to account for this by coming up with the concept of a multiverse. According to this idea, our universe, unique among an infinite number of other universes, just happened to have all the right laws of physics to create it and sustain it.

That would explain it then. Only it doesn't. Suffice to say that the multiverse theory does not come from long calculations chalked up on a university blackboard. It is nothing more than a wild guess, plucked out of thin air, bereft of any supporting evidence, in fact *without any possibility of supporting evidence* since any data for it, being beyond our universe, can only exist outside our ability to locate it and test it.

This is the poverty of the kind of option you're left with if you have an *a priori* assumption of the impossibility of a creator God. This is the best alternative that the most brilliant human minds on the planet can offer for the creation of everything from nothing.

It doesn't help the atheist case at all. It just kicks the can further down the road. I am not an expert but this just looks like philosophical desperation to me; the kind that must allow for the possibility -since there has to be an infinite number of universes- of another cosmos somewhere where flying unicorns and candy floss telephones orbit the planet of the fairies.

John Lennox's birthday cake still needs an explanation of who baked it, who it was baked for and why. All we can really do is look at each other, shrug our shoulders and note that it is there. And then enjoy eating it.

And I am still looking in vain for an intellectually satisfying explanation as to why it is *more logical*, not less, that our vast, mysterious, complex and astonishingly beautiful universe came into being from nothing, all by itself, and not by the will of an all-powerful creator who is outside of time and has no beginning and no end.

That's why "In the beginning God created the heavens and the earth" (Genesis 1.1) sounds like a decent starting point to me.

And that's the first reason why I think Christianity can't be written off as a silly fantasy.

Chapter 2

ACROSS THE UNIVERSE

Maths was never my strongest subject at school and I am embarrassed to admit that I still struggle with my times tables now. So anything to do with numbers is a bit of a challenge for me - and the more zeroes there are the worse it gets. I am standing on the shoulders of giants here when I say that **the fine tuning of the universe suggests high level engineering, by an intelligent being - not a fluke of complete randomness.**

What do I mean when I talk about fine tuning in the universe? I mean, according to the calculations of people who are clever enough to work these things out, that the cosmic physics from the very earliest moments after the Big Bang to the present day have to be incredibly exact to work at all.

For example, at the dawn of time there had to be a very, very precisely fine balance between the outward thrust of the exploding universe and the gravitational force that pulls matter together.

Professor Paul Davies of Arizona State University has stated that the correlation of outward thrust and gravitational pull needed to be "accurate to a staggering one part in 10 to the power of 60. That is to say, had the explosion differed in strength at the outset by only one part in 10, 000, 000, 000, 000, 000, 000, 000, 000, 000, 000, 000, 000, 000, 000, 000, 000, 000, 000, 000, 000 [there are sixty zeros after the ten] the universe we now perceive would not exist. To give some meaning to these numbers, suppose you wanted to fire a bullet at a one-inch target on the other side of the observable universe, twenty billion light years away. Your aim would have to be accurate to that same one part in 10 to the power of 60."[4] That's the guy I'd pick in my paintballing team.

Furthermore, the density of the infant universe also had to be calibrated to an almost unimaginable exactitude.

Consider this quotation from Professor Stephen Hawking of Cambridge University: "If the density of the universe one second after the Big Bang had been greater by one part in 1, 000, 000, 000, 000 [a thousand billion], the universe would have recollapsed after ten years. On the other hand, if the density of the universe at that time had been less by the same amount, the universe would have been essentially empty since it was about ten years old. How is it that the density of the universe was chosen with such precision? Perhaps there is some reason why the universe has exactly the right density."[5]

But it's not just at the start of time that the sums absolutely had to add up. They have had to be exactly right as time has gone on as well. Professor Michael Poole, of Kings College London, further underlined the incredible fine tuning needed for a viable universe by stating that gravity has to have the exact force it does have if stars (and therefore complex elements necessary for life) were ever to have formed at all.

"Out of the Big Bang there came mostly the lightest gases, hydrogen and helium. These needed to be fused together to cook up the heavier elements like carbon, nitrogen and oxygen which are the building blocks of life. The high temperature, high pressure conditions found in the interior of stars provide the ovens for doing this. Some stars then blow up when they are old, scattering these heavier elements into space, eventually making up our bodies. But how do stars form in the first place? Through gravity compressing a cloud of gas, heating it in the process and igniting the nuclear fusion fires. Make gravity any weaker, and the stars will not ignite. Make it any stronger, and the stars will be so massive they will burn too fast and long-lived stars like the Sun will not exist."[6]

So the *exact* force of the outward thrust of the Big Bang, the *exact* density of all matter in the universe and the *exact* strength of gravitational pull are three examples of some ultra-precise calibration that has to be absolutely perfect for any universe to (1) come into being at all and (2) continue to expand and develop.

I do not have the training or expertise to either affirm or challenge these assertions. I am a layman, not a scientist. I read this kind of thing as an interested amateur - and frankly I am awed by what I find.

For some curious reason, the physics and mathematics of the beginnings of our universe are very, very exact and without that precision we would have no universe, no stars, no matter, no life, no anything.

Like my first reason for being a Christian, all I have said so far proves nothing at all. Indeed on its own it is like a God of the gaps argument (answering every so far unresolved scientific question with the answer "It must be God" rather than testing the data to try and work it out).

But I think Hawking's question "How is it that the density of the universe was so precisely chosen?" needs a better answer than "Someone got lucky and won the lottery jackpot three times in a row and amazingly it was us." If a value is "chosen" to quote

Professor Hawking, I naturally want to ask "*How* was it chosen?" and also "Did someone choose it and if so, who did?"

It is interesting to me that the Bible does not merely claim that God created the heavens and the earth by commanding that light should appear (Genesis 1.1), it also affirms that he progressively developed his work (Genesis 1.2-27) and asserts that he goes on sustaining it, holding it all together for his pleasure and by his will (Colossians 1.16-17). To me, that is a basic working model that matches what we know from science and makes some sense of the highly improbable maths.

It would be silly to claim that the Bible is a scientific textbook - it clearly isn't. Nor incidentally is a book of poems, a public information notice, a dictionary, a historical novel, a newspaper report, a tweet or a car maintenance handbook. People interpret what they read in ways appropriate to the genre in question. That does not mean that poems, novels, reports and tweets etc. cannot express *truth* in their own context, and I want to argue that this is the case for the Bible too.

In my view, what cosmologists have learned about the fine tuning of the universe does not do away with the necessity of creative intelligence that the Bible affirms. On the contrary, it seems to me that if we must discount any possibility of intelligent supervision over the formation of our universe the coincidences are much too implausible. The sums just don't add up.

How could it have all happened without God? Professor Paul Davies again (he is not a Christian incidentally), for all his brilliance, seems out of ideas and admits that it certainly *looks like* some kind of creator had to have been involved: "It is hard to resist the impression that the present structure of the universe, apparently so sensitive to minor alterations in numbers, has been rather carefully thought out. The seemingly miraculous concurrence of these numerical values must remain the most compelling evidence for cosmic design."[7]

Sir Fred Hoyle, to whom we owe the term 'Big Bang', confessed that his atheism was greatly shaken by all this. "Would you not say to yourself, 'Some super-calculating intellect must have designed the properties of the carbon atom', otherwise the chance of my finding such an atom through the blind forces of nature would be utterly minuscule. A common sense interpretation of the facts suggests that a superintellect has monkeyed with physics, as well as with chemistry and biology, and that there are no blind forces worth speaking about in nature. The numbers one calculates from the facts seem to me so overwhelming as to put this conclusion almost beyond question" he said in 1981.[8]

And finally, in *A Brief History of Time*, Stephen Hawking (as is well known, he's not a Christian either) wrote "This means that the initial state of the universe must have been very carefully chosen indeed if the hot Big Bang model is correct back to the beginning of time. It would be very difficult to explain why the universe should have begun in this way except as an act of a god who intended to create beings like us."[9]

Well, yes. And yet, on their own, these awesome discoveries would be insufficient to convince me that Christianity must be true. I would have to be very closed-minded if it didn't at least set me thinking though.

The 26 reasons I listed *taken together* have led me to that conclusion. If the arithmetic in this chapter, has left you blurry eyed, the next one is perhaps a little more down to earth.

Chapter 3

NO PLACE LIKE HOME

If there were even a little variation, the tiniest modification to the conditions we have on Earth, intelligent life as we know it would not be possible at all. **The dimensions, properties, proportions and situation of the Earth appear to have been carefully and wisely chosen.**

Ever since we human beings have realised we live on a spinning watery rock and looked up to the heavens at other moving spheres we have wondered if we are alone in the universe. Could intelligent life or even microscopic, unicellular, bacterial life have developed anywhere else?

Relatively recently, the Kepler telescope has discovered planets in other solar systems and has been able to work out if, due to their size, their distance from their star and their probable elemental constitution, they are the type of planets that might be able to support life.

At the 221st meeting of the American Astronomical Society in California in January 2013 astronomers announced that perhaps one in six stars hosts an Earth-sized planet in a close orbit.

I have no more idea whether extra-terrestrial life exists than anyone else of course. One would imagine that the chances are quite high. But the conditions necessary for complex life forms like human beings appear to be many and varied. Our Earth seems uncannily well suited to provide for us a good home.

Seven different factors, each very precisely just right, favour the emergence and sustenance of life on Earth. (Bill Bryson, in his excellent book *A Short History of Nearly Everything* says there are forty factors but you will be relieved to read that I'm sticking to just seven!)[10]

Firstly, our distance from the Sun (about 150 million kilometres or 8 light-minutes away) happens to be *just right*. Our nearest neighbour towards the Sun, Venus, (about 41 million kilometres closer) has a surface temperature of about 450°C. Our nearest neighbour away from the Sun, Mars, plunges to -140°C at its coldest.

Bryson comments that if Earth were just 5% nearer the Sun or 15% further away from it, we would no longer be situated in a habitable zone. A shade closer to our star (in cosmological terms) and the oceans would boil.

A little further away and our good Earth would be an inhospitable ball of rock and ice.

As Goldilocks noted, one bowl of porridge was too hot, one was too cold but one was just right. The Earth's properties being just right for life, and not just in the area of surface temperature, it has what some have called the Goldilocks Effect.

Secondly, Earth happens to spin round a star that is *just* the *right* sort. Though it may seem odd, bigger stars burn their fuel much more quickly. But stars like the Sun have enough hydrogen and helium to last about ten billion years so we're not even half way through our energy supply yet.

Astronomer Dr. Guillermo Gonzalez and Philosopher of Science Dr. Jay Richards have said it would take a star with the highly particular properties of our Sun; the right mass, the right light, the right age, the right distance, the right orbit, the right galaxy and the right location in the galaxy to nurture living organisms on an orbiting planet.[11]

Thirdly, the size of the Earth is *just right* to support a life- sustaining atmosphere. By contrast, the Moon, for example, is too small a sphere so its weaker gravitational attraction fails to hold any gases to its surface. Having an atmosphere is absolutely vital to us, way beyond supplying us with breathable air. It warms the surface of the planet through the greenhouse effect. It has a layer of ozone which filters out harmful solar radiation. It burns up all but the largest and rarest asteroids heading our way. And it evens out temperature scales between night and day (one reason why the scale is so wide-ranging on Mars is that its atmosphere is much thinner).

Fourthly, our Earth's mix and quantities of key elements, especially an abundance of liquid water at the surface is *just right*. By contrast Venus, for example, is largely sulphurous at the surface and with a dense atmosphere of carbon dioxide and clouds of sulphuric acid. If space tourism ever ends up offering a full-board fortnight on Venus you can bet people will be complaining about their holiday from hell on Trip Advisor! Only 0.05% of the earth's crust is carbon but that's enough – in fact, *just enough*. Life is not possible without it but too much of it in the atmosphere is a very bad thing as we keep hearing on the news. It's why Venus has a runaway greenhouse effect and an atmosphere hot enough to melt lead.

Fifthly, also unlike Venus, our Earth has *just* the *right* foundation in its depths; a solid iron centre and convection currents in the liquid iron outer core. The ferric interior of our planet makes the Earth a massive magnet with a vast magnetic field that extends as far as the Moon. Without this magnetic field, our atmosphere would slowly erode altogether through solar wind (sudden and massive bursts of energy from the Sun's atmosphere). As Chris Wickham writes: "The only thing stopping Earth having a lifeless environment like Mars is the magnetic field that shields us from deadly solar radiation."[12]

Sixthly, the conditions on our Earth's crust are *just right*; we have plate tectonics. Our planet's surface is constantly shifting. The outer crust is made up of vast slabs of land that move towards and away from each other. There is a growing conviction among planetary scientists that plate tectonics are necessary for life because they replenish the nutrition that primitive life depends on and recycle carbon around the planet. Not only that, but plate tectonics, over many, many years, elevate landmasses and produce mountainous regions. This is vital to us because if the land on our planet were uniformly flat, it would all be submerged under about 4 kilometres of sea.

Seventhly, our Earth inhabits a solar system with *just the right* mix of planets and satellites, notably a moon; the largest satellite in the solar system in relation to its host planet. The Moon is *just right* in terms of size and distance from Earth to stabilize our planet's axial tilt so avoiding significant, rapid and life-threatening climate changes. The absence of a moon for Mars has been the other main cause of fluctuations in temperature spanning 180°C. Our moon is big enough and close enough to command tidal flows around our coasts but not so big or so near that the tides completely engulf our landmasses every time the Moon passes above us. Not only this, but when the Apollo missions orbited the

Moon and gave us our first views of its dark side, the face that is always turned away from us, we saw that it is much more pockmarked by craters than the side we see. That's because it has been hit far more often by space rocks slamming into it. In other words, the Moon is an excellent shield, defending us from many disastrous and life-threatening asteroid impacts. Jupiter's powerful gravity (its mass adds up to two and a half times all the other planets put together) is also highly effective in dragging asteroids away from our path. According to Eric Metaxas writing in *The Wall Street Journal*, "a thousand times as many would hit Earth's surface" if Jupiter were absent from our solar system.[13]

Of course, some say that this view is the wrong way round and that life has simply adapted itself to the conditions available on our planet. But if that were true wouldn't we surely have discovered abundant life elsewhere in space adapting to conditions there?

In short, I marvel that our planet pulsates with life because it is *just right* for life to thrive. We take for granted how well life flourishes on Earth. But if any of the features listed above were a fraction different from what they are, life as we know it would not be possible here. Like the instantaneous creation of everything from nothing (chapter 1) and the incredibly precise physics necessary for it all to happen (chapter 2) it all appears to have been carefully arranged.

> *For this is what the Lord says—*
> *he who created the heavens, he is God;*
> *he who fashioned and made the earth,*
> *he founded it; he did not create it to be empty,*
> *but formed it to be inhabited—*
> *he says: "I am the Lord, and there is no other."*
>
> Isaiah 45.18.

Again, these things, taken in isolation, would certainly never be anywhere near enough to convince me that Christianity is true, or even that God exists.

As former professor of Mathematical Physics at the University of Cambridge and Anglican clergyman John Polkinghorne put it: "A big, fundamental question, like belief in God (or disbelief), is not settled by a single argument. It's too complicated for that. What one has to do is to consider lots of different issues and see whether or not the answers one gets add up to a total picture that makes sense."[14]

I agree. But, though it is an improbable marvel that any planet with exactly the right conditions for flourishing life exists at all, the greater wonder by far is that even the very simplest life forms could emerge from non-living components. That's what the next chapter is about.

Chapter 4

THAT'S LIFE

To sum up where we have got to so far, pause to consider these assertions from the world of science if you will: (1) With no raw materials to work from, at the beginning of time, everything in the universe inexplicably and instantaneously just started to exist. (2) The physics necessary for everything coming into being and to continue existing have to be mind-bogglingly precise. (3) For the Earth to be in any position to support flourishing life conditions need to be exceptionally well calibrated and it just so happens that they are fine-tuned to astonishing precision.

And now (4) How do you pull off the staggeringly complex feat of getting dead matter -completely unassisted- to become complex, self-multiplying organisms? **The unlikely story of the appearance of life on our planet points to the work of an author.**

If all that doesn't make us wonder, maybe we should wonder why.

In short, to embrace naturalism (the belief that nature is all there is and there is no spiritual realm and no possibility of a supernatural being) you have to argue that:

- Nothing created everything
- Chaos produced precision fine-tuning
- Non-life gave birth to life
- Unconsciousness brought consciousness into being

Good luck with that!

Could even the simplest life forms have come into existence, all by themselves, from inanimate –stone dead- components? And if so, how did they do it? (And incidentally, if life could and did just spontaneously materialize from inanimate matter why is the resurrection of Jesus from the dead so far-fetched? But that's for another chapter).

How life was ever derived from non-life is the biggest conundrum in biology. It made the staunchly atheist philosopher Anthony Flew think the unthinkable. "It has become inordinately difficult to even to begin to think about a naturalistic theory of the evolution of that first reproducing organism" he confessed. Flew ended up abandoning atheism altogether and writing a book called *There is a God: How the World's Most Notorious Atheist Changed His Mind.*[15]

The problem that unsettled Flew's curious mind is summed up well by Professor of Genetics at Harvard Medical School Jack W. Szostak and biochemist Dr. Alonso Ricardo: "It is virtually impossible to imagine how a cell's machines, which are mostly protein-based catalysts called enzymes, could have formed spontaneously as life first arose from nonliving matter around 3.7 billion years ago. To be sure, under the right conditions some building blocks of proteins, the amino acids, form easily from simpler chemicals, as Stanley L. Miller and Harold C. Urey of the University of Chicago discovered in pioneering experiments in the 1950s. But going from there to proteins and enzymes is a different matter."[16]

Proteins and enzymes and DNA are exceptionally complex molecules that just do not self-create any more than laptop computers self-assemble or cardigans self-knit. Flew admitted the folly of going on pretending that they do.

Biochemists have tried simulating the formation of life from non-life with the most advanced experiments in high-tech laboratories and they cannot get anywhere near it. If our most intelligent minds cannot pull it off in the most sophisticated conditions, should we not be sceptical when we are told that it managed all by itself on a messy and primitive Earth?

Geneticist Dr. Michael Denton, who describes himself as an agnostic, explains why we should not be surprised that this quest to replicate the creation of life has always ended in disappointment. "Between a living cell and the most highly ordered non-biological systems, such as a crystal or a snowflake, there is a chasm as vast and absolute as it is possible to conceive. Even the tiniest of bacterial cells is a veritable micro-miniaturised factory containing thousands of exquisitely designed pieces of intricate molecular machinery, made up altogether of 100 thousand million atoms, far more complicated than any machine built by man and absolutely without parallel in the non-living world."[17]

No wonder open-minded atheists like Anthony Flew and Alister McGrath, who followed where the evidence leads, found this so troublesome to their prior assumptions. Honest sceptics know they cannot claim that the appearance of living organisms points to the non-existence of God. On the contrary, when they look at the evidence objectively, some reluctantly concede that the case for some kind of creator seems overwhelming.

Personally, I think the notion of a wise, all-powerful God is as reasonable as anything else that has been suggested. It fits with the fact of our inexplicably well calibrated universe and with God's self-revelation in the Bible where he is referred to as "the Author of Life" (Acts 3.15).

> *The God who made the world and everything in it is the Lord of heaven and earth... he himself gives everyone life and breath and everything else.*
> Acts 17.24-25.

To sum up, here's the deal to get life from non-life: twenty different amino acids are involved in producing proteins and they have to be arranged, often duplicated, in precisely the right place in the protein molecule.

According to Oxford Professor of Mathematics John Lennox, in *God's Undertaker* "If we had a pool consisting of all twenty the probability of getting the correct amino acid at a specific site in the protein would be 1/20. Thus the probability of getting 100 amino acids in the correct order would be (1/20) to the power of 100, which is 1 in 10 with 130 zeros after it. But this is just the start... For these calculations concern only a single protein. Yet life as we know it requires hundreds of thousands of proteins, and it has been calculated that the odds against producing these by chance is more than 10 with 40,000 zeros after it to 1."[18]

The numbers say it loud and clear; random chance is not a satisfactory explanation for the origins of life on Earth. Like a detective who arrives at a crime scene and says "This was no accident" we need to look for a cause.

PARENTHESIS: WHAT ABOUT EVOLUTION?

At this point, some will be asking themselves "What about evolution then?" This particular issue is important because it is such a stumbling block to belief in God for so many.

If anyone looks at evidence from the fossil record, from genetic research, from biogeography etc. with an open mind and follows where it leads they will have to conclude that it is very highly likely that species are related to each other and have undergone modification over great periods of time. There are small numbers of Christians who disagree. I respect them and, who knows, it may be that they end up being correct, but I don't think so. The argument for an ancient universe and natural selection is compelling and as a Christian who believes the Bible is trustworthy and inspired I say that without embarrassment.

It is regrettable that the debate about our origins has become so polarised and reductionist in some circles. It is as if there are only two choices available to us; we must accept that we are the result of a random, godless accident in a meaningless universe or we must sign up to a literal six 24-hour day creation narrative and contend that the Earth is as young as 6,000 years old.

In fact, most -not all, but most- Christians I know accept that there has been descent with modification in living species over long periods of time without any erosion whatsoever of their belief in God or in the Bible as God's word.

The two narratives, creation and evolution, can coexist perfectly happily. Consider this analogy; when Christians marvel at God's handiwork after a baby is born, they do not deny that it required sexual intercourse between the child's mother and father to cause the pregnancy. Nor do they see the parents' role as proving the inexistence of God. No, the idea of divine direction of natural processes makes perfect sense to Christians.

If Christianity were really anti-science there would be no Christians going anywhere near it. David Robertson in his book *The Dawkins Letters* lists Asa Gray (botanist), Charles Walcott (palaeontologist), Theodosius Dobzhansky (evolutionary biologist), RJ Berry (geneticist), Owen Gingerich (scientific historian) and Francis Collins (Head of the Human Genome Project) as but a few examples of internationally distinguished scientists who are also Christian believers.[19] There are many more of course. Christians in Science has over 1,000 members including senior scientists engaged in research and development, university lecturers and scientific writers. The idea that science and faith are incompatible is simply false. Incidentally, the popular notion of an overwhelming rejection of Darwin's *Origin of Species* from the Church in the 19th Century is an urban myth as has been pointed out on the television show QI.

As has often been said, science asks "how". Faith explores "why." It is a category error to force science to explain *why* life appeared or say the Bible was written primarily to tell us *how* it occurred down to every last detail.

How should people read the Bible, especially Genesis, then on questions related to science? By acknowledging the nuances of ancient Hebrew literary genre and interpreting Genesis with due attention to its context. Most Christians I know do this. That does not at all interfere with the belief that Genesis is truth revealed by God. Genesis 1 is *theological* truth, telling us things about God, but presenting them in the genre of an epic narrative.

Consider this comparison: We know Julius Caesar really existed, living from 100BC to 44BC. Shakespeare's brilliant play about his life is a broadly accurate depiction of the great turning points of his life. But no one would seriously claim that the object of the play is to reproduce verbatim the historical dialogue between Caesar, Brutus and Mark Antony.

Any critic who rejected the play because some of its verbal exchanges might not be absolutely factual would miss the point. Shakespeare's genius and inspiration is to bring out themes like power, free will, fate, loyalty and betrayal for his audience to reflect on through the framework of real history.

I think we are meant to understand Genesis 1 in a similar way. The first chapter in the Bible tells me about God's *ex-nihilo* creative power, his careful ordering of the universe, his wise authorship of life on earth and the special place humankind has in his creative plan, unique over all other animal life. Bringing everything that exists into being was effortless for God. As he might say, "It was all in a week's work to me."

In short, Genesis 1 is a beautiful artist's impression that explains the divine reason why everything is as it is, who is behind it all, and in language any child can understand.

Who knows, the theory of evolution may one day be demonstrated to be fatally flawed and false but I think, at the present time, it offers the best explanation for the mechanics of natural history we have.

But it absolutely does not explain *everything*. For example, if all evolution is a slow process of mutations, we should surely expect fossil excavations to show us every phase between two related species. In fact, we get thousands of examples of two apparently related species but they both appear all at once and fully formed in the fossil record. It's relatively easy to dig up a hadrosaur skeleton. There are many examples. But where are the equally abundant pre-hadrosaurs that came before? Evolution seems to happen in sudden jumps, not in a slow, uniform glide.

I do not offer this example as an attack against evolution. It just contributes to my nagging scepticism about evolution as *the* mechanism that explains *everything*. It doesn't quite. In particular, one step back from natural selection, which I accept, evolution fails to account for the origin of life itself which is the main point I have tried to make in chapter 4. In a nutshell, natural selection absolutely does not explain how or why there is anything to select in the first place. Nor does it score a God-does-not-exist open goal.

Bill Bryson writes (we're back to cakes again): "It is rather as if all the ingredients in your kitchen somehow got together and baked themselves into a cake – but a cake that could moreover divide when necessary to produce more cakes. It is little wonder that we call it the miracle of life." [20]

And what of the great chasm that exists between human beings and all other animals? True, 97% of our DNA is identical to a chimpanzee's but we share 60% of a fruit fly's DNA too!

Similar percentages of resemblance may be observed between different models of car designed and built by the same manufacturer. That doesn't mean that those differences must have occurred by themselves. No one denies that they are due to someone with a drawing board. Manifestly, they are.

And that 3% that distinguishes us from our nearest genetic cousin... our consciousness, our search for meaning, our appreciation of art and beauty and greatness, our facility for love, our yearning for the divine, our capacity for selfless philanthropy and noble self-sacrifice, our intelligence that has propelled us to the Moon, our love of organised sport, our ability to reason, to feel shame, to be moved to tears by music, to smile and laugh and hope…

All these set us in a category apart. They point to the Image of God in us, which is where we will travel to in the next chapter.

Chapter 5

SOUL TO SOUL

What if the yearning for meaning in the human heart is because we live in a meaningful universe? But if there is purpose in the universe where did it come from? And if there is no God, is anything ultimately significant?

The next three chapters leave those improbably long numbers mind-boggling cosmic factoids behind us and find us leaning over chin-on-fist, thinking profound things. This is going to be more to do with metaphysics than physics. Ladies and gentlemen, I give you the deep mysteries of the human condition.

One of the endlessly repeated Richard Dawkins quotes that do the rounds is the one from *River Out of Eden* (1995) in which he says: "The universe we observe has precisely the properties we should expect if there is, at bottom, no design, no purpose, no evil and no good, nothing but blind pitiless indifference."[21]

OK. But the question this raises is obvious: if the universe really is purposeless, blind and indifferent, where does Dawkins' evident enthusiasm for purpose, insight and understanding come from? Do people long for something that does not exist? And where would that longing spring from in a blind, pitilessly indifferent cosmos?

That's why I think that **the human soul's yearning for meaning points to the existence of intelligence and meaning in the universe. And the existence of intelligence and meaning in the universe points to the existence of an intelligent and meaningful God.**

What is it that marks us human beings out from all other beasts? We, like them, eat, sleep, procreate, and defend ourselves from danger. But unlike them, we know the difference between knowledge and wisdom. We have an existential awareness of ourselves. We explore the nature of our existence, asking "Who am I?", "Where do I come from?" and "Why am I here?" We appreciate artistic beauty and symbolism. We have a sense of our mortality. We need meaning and purpose in our lives. We have an innate aspiration for significance. There is a spiritual side to us. For all these reasons, we are not the same as other beasts. Because of these differences, human life is sacred.

I'd say we have a soul. "Soul" is a difficult word to define. It's like the essence of a person, the self. It is what makes me *me* and you *you*. Where is the soul then? It isn't anywhere really. Like the love I have for my friends, and like the psyche it isn't hemmed in by a physical location. But I know I love, and I know I have a psyche, or a consciousness, just as much as I have a brain. And I feel I have a soul just as much as I have a body.

Distinguished Professor of Philosophy at Biola University in La Mirada, California J. P. Moreland has defined consciousness as "Our introspection, sensations, thoughts, emotions, desires, beliefs, and free choices that make us alive and aware. The 'soul' contains our consciousness and animates our body" he says.[22]

Radio journalist John Humphrys tried to articulate this in his book *In God We Doubt: Confessions of a Failed Atheist*:

> "Biologists like Richard Dawkins know a thousand times more than most of us ever will about how our bodies work and how we evolved… But there is that other mysterious attribute, about which so many scientists are curiously incurious. There is our soul, our spirit, our conscience or whatever else you want to call it… We sense a spiritual element in that nobility and in the miracle of unselfish love and sacrifice, something beyond our conscious understanding."[23]

The Judaeo-Christian understanding of this phenomenon is that we are more than a tidily arranged ensemble of atoms and molecules and we are not just another species alongside all the others. We are created in the image of God.

Saint Augustine's famous prayer "You have formed us for yourself, and our hearts are restless till they find rest in you" gives voice to this. It shows that this existential yearning was known and felt in the 3rd Century so it is not a new phenomenon. And it is all the more striking that it was written by an intellectual giant who, as a young man, lived a wild and hedonistic lifestyle. His lavishly promiscuous youth left him empty handed and still searching for something more.

Bertrand Russell was a leading atheist in the mid-20th Century. He wrote an essay called *Why I Am Not a Christian*. But tellingly, when his daughter Katharine Tait wrote a biography of her father she wrote:

> "Somewhere in the back of my father's mind and at the bottom of his heart, in the depths of his soul, there was an empty space that had once been filled by God and he never found anything else to put in it."[24]

I think most people would admit that they have a restless sense of something deep down that is not satisfied by any material thing. The pleasure gained by any new purchase, however eagerly awaited beforehand, soon wears off. That suggests that the soul can only be fulfilled by something less tangible than the stuff we accumulate.

I find it striking (but unsurprising) that, in a century that has seen the cultural influence of Christianity recede in the U.K. - influenced by Russell's atheism - unhappiness in marriage leading to family breakdown and world-weariness leading to drug abuse and excessive eating and drinking are at record levels. When our souls are starved of meaning and purpose our relationships become unfulfilling and we seek escape from the inevitable emptiness we are left with.

The Christian apologist Ravi Zacharias once fielded questions from an auditorium of University students in the USA. He had been commending the case for God and, as is the way, had received a frosty reception. One student raised his hand and stated that Mr Zacharias had been wasting his time talking about real meaning in life because there is no meaning in life. "Everything is meaningless."

Zacharias asked the young man to stand and replied, "Sir, I take it that when you claim 'everything is meaningless', you assume that what you have just said is meaning*ful*. If your statement really is meaning*ful* then everything is therefore not meaning*less*, and you have unwittingly demonstrated your statement to be false. But if you still

==maintain that everything is meaning*less*, including your statement, by your own criteria you have essentially said nothing of consequence and you may sit down."==

Alright, perhaps it was a little unkind to the student to so devastatingly expose the inherent weakness of his argument. But the point is that everything is not meaningless. It can just feel that way when people deny their soul the oxygen it needs to thrive.

There are many ways this image of God expresses itself but for now I just want to say that some kind of spiritual expression is practically universal – and seems innate.

Swedish-American author John Ortberg writes about a little girl who asked her atheist father "Who made me?" The father started to talk about the Big Bang, random mutations, blind chance and the absurdities of this vastly meaningless universe. She listened to him and looked down at her shoes, a little disappointed. Then the father said, in the interests of balance, "Oh, and there are some other silly people who believe in an all-powerful being called *God* and that he loves everyone and that he made us all." The little girl started to dance around the room shouting excitedly, "I knew what you told me wasn't true! It's him, it's him!"[25]

What is it in the human soul that, in all civilisations, in all history, seems to draw so many to a sense that there is something - Someone - greater than oneself to worship? Even in cultures that violently suppress or relentlessly attack this view, for example the Soviet Union and the 21st Century Western world, nothing seems to be able to snuff out this spiritual flame in the human soul. Could it be because we are made in the image of a God who is worthy of praise and worship?

This not only makes sense to me, it helps me to make sense of the world around me. As CS Lewis so memorably put it "I believe in Christianity as I believe that the sun has risen, not only because I see it, but because by it I see everything else."[26]

The Bible expresses it this way:

> *[God] has made everything beautiful in its time. He has also set eternity in the human heart; yet no one can fathom what God has done from beginning to end.*
> Ecclesiastes 3.11.

In other words, human beings instinctively sense there is an eternal, spiritual dimension to life, though they may suppress such feelings, but can never work it all out with their finite minds.

Those who reject this vision of the human condition tell us that our existence is just an unlikely fluke; we are all alone, having arrived completely by chance in a universe that has no design, no destination, no point and no meaning. I think they need to explain, better than they have so far, why human beings are so evidently on a restless quest to interpret deeper meaning, and discover an overarching structure in life, the universe and everything.

They need to tell us why we seem hard-wired to probe the realities of our existence and see meaningful patterns there. They need to enlighten us as to why people ask themselves "What's it all for?" They need to account for the reason why people so often ask themselves "Is there more to life than this?" especially when they seem to have everything they need or could want. Maybe we do live in a universe with "no purpose… nothing but blind pitiless indifference." But it doesn't seem like it; quite the opposite.

As CS Lewis (again) once wrote in *Mere Christianity*, "Creatures are not born with desires unless satisfaction for those desires exists. A baby feels hunger: well, there is such a thing as food. A duckling wants to swim: well, there is such a thing as water. Men feel sexual desire: well, there is such a thing as sex. If I find in myself a desire which no experience in this world can satisfy, the most probable explanation is that I was made for another world."[27]

Exactly.

Or as Philanthropist Sir John Templeton put it: "Would it not be strange if a universe without purpose accidentally created humans who are so obsessed with purpose?"[28]

Strange indeed...

Chapter 6

GOOD AND BAD

When our children were very small, Kathie and I could guarantee one thing; if everything went quiet for more than about a minute, our offspring had either inexplicably fallen asleep or were up to something they knew full well was not really allowed. Like drawing on the wall using cat food as paint. They knew about right and wrong well before they could walk and were experts in challenging us to define where the boundaries lay.

Where do human beings get this right and wrong thing from? That would be a weird anomaly in a universe that had no truth, no ultimate good, no such thing as evil, and where everything was relative. **The fact that we have a conscience at all, a sense of right and wrong, points to the existence of a moral universe governed by a good God.**

Mark Twain once said "Man is the only animal that blushes. Or needs to."[29] So why do we, unlike all other beasts, have an inbuilt sense of good and evil? I wonder where this comes from.

An inbuilt moral compass seems unique to human beings, and forms part of the Judaeo-Christian understanding of being made in the image of God. We are morally responsible creatures with our eyes opened to knowing right and wrong. We celebrate virtue and we deplore foul play.

Animals, by contrast, instinctively know only of what is favourable to their survival. For example, it is not a lion's *fault* if it attacks and devours the cubs of a male rival. He does what comes naturally to him and there is no question of "guilt" or "vice" or "sin." I'll say more about this in the next chapter.

But if a man wanders next door with an axe and kills all the children in the house there is justifiable outrage, whatever the motive. We all know it is *wrong*, full-stop.

Part of the humanist response to claims that we live in a moral universe is to object to the use of words like "evil". But the kind of horrors human beings seem uniquely capable of (for example, the incarceration of a young woman by her father as a sex slave in Austria, the summary execution of men and boys in Srebrenica, the abduction, torture and murder by 10 year-old boys of a toddler in Liverpool and the flying of hijacked airplanes into skyscrapers in Manhattan) are not just "inappropriate" or "unacceptable." These words are patently inadequate to describe acts that are morally wrong and sick.

Some people who are disinclined to believe in God say that what we call 'right' and 'wrong' is simply learned values picked up from the ambient culture. We are informed by our environment, so the argument goes, that certain things are OK and that certain things are not.

But from about the time children learn to talk, parents are given regular updates from their offspring about what they judge to be morally right. "It's" "not" and "fair" are often the first three words children learn to put together! Our sense of justice seems hard-wired from birth.

Isn't this surely just the way things are? Imagine living in a land where an individual took pride in stealing from the nurses who had cared for his or her dying mother. Imagine a world where parents eating their undernourished children's dinner was admired by all.

We know *instinctively* that such behaviour is wrong.

When Homer Simpson sells the ride-on lawnmower he'd borrowed from Flanders on e-Bay to fund a month's supply of beer and donuts he might find a way of justifying it, especially after a few hours in Moe's bar. But even Homer knows deep down that he is probably a bit out of order.

CS Lewis has shown in *The Abolition of Man* that ==the basic standards of morality, of what people know to be right and wrong, are more or less the same in all cultures and at all times.== This gives real weight to the argument that ==objective good and evil are self-evident.==

But what if our sense of morality derives from an evolved desire for the common good (giving our species a better chance of survival)? According to this view, racial prejudice, jealousy, cruelty to animals, bullying, adultery, theft and computer hacking are *not objectively wrong*. They are just what we have collectively decided at the present time to say is against our interests as a species.

CS Lewis again, this time in *Mere Christianity* puts it best: "If we ask: 'Why ought I to be unselfish?' and you reply 'Because it is good for society,' we may then ask, 'Why should I care what's good for society except when it happens to pay *me* personally?' and you then have to say, 'Because you *ought* to be unselfish' - which simply brings us back to where we started. You are saying what is true but you are not getting any further."[30]

No, ethical standards are surely etched onto the human soul. Our conscience marks us out from all other beasts as morally responsible beings. Right and wrong are real concepts in a moral universe because God, who is wholly good and just in all he does, has created us in his image.

If there is no God, there can be no *absolute* standard of good and evil. This is not to say that atheists cannot be good people. Of course they can and often are. It means rather that they have no basis for their moral code. They have to borrow one - and they do so mostly from the Judeo-Christian tradition.

Even Richard Dawkins has had to admit that the quest for absolute standards of right and wrong - which exclude the existence of God - is doomed to failure: "It is pretty hard to defend absolute morals on anything other than religious grounds"[31] he writes. It's rare I say this, but I am glad to agree with Professor Dawkins on this occasion.

Make no mistake, if there is no God it's your morality against mine - and there are no measures, no standards, no criteria to determine which of us is right. There *is* no "right."

One of us might think that killing old people, or disabled people, or some foetuses, is fine because they are a burden on society or an inconvenience to individuals. And one of us might say that it is wrong *because it is wrong* (ultimately because all human life is created in the image of God and therefore should be treated with respect and dignity from the beginning of life to its end). Let's just hope that if and when our own loved ones become acutely disabled, the good guys are making the rules.

To sum up, if a good God who opposes evil exists, then whether we believe in him or not, we should expect that all human beings would have a hard-wired sense of morality – which is, in fact, exactly what we observe.

As the Apostle Paul put it:

> *When outsiders who have never heard of God's law follow it more or less by instinct, they confirm its truth by their obedience. They show that God's law is not something alien, imposed on us from without, but woven into the very fabric of our creation. There is something deep within them that echoes God's yes and no, right and wrong.*
>
> Romans 2.14-15, (The Message).

This is another area incidentally, where science, for all its greatness, is of no help to us at all. Scientific research gave birth to both penicillin and the atomic bomb. It is powerless as a giver or measure of moral values. Science tells me that if I inject your sandwiches with arsenic you will die eating them. Science cannot tell me that I would be wrong to do so.

Bottom line: rightness and wrongness are only discernible by the human soul made in the image of a just and holy God to whom everyone will one day be required to give an account. That's the sixth reason why Christianity makes good sense.

Chapter 7

WHAT'S WRONG?

Something is wrong with the world. I take this as self-evident and beyond dispute. It's plain to see. Everywhere you go on our planet there is injustice, hatred, cruelty, corruption, rejection and untold other evils. Why does it have to be this way? Is this what any of us would actually choose? Surely not. I think that it's only in the world of theology that an accurate diagnosis of what's wrong with the world (and what the cure is) can be found.

The best explanation I have found of what's evidently wrong with the world is that there is a universal and inescapable downward tug on the human soul. The Bible calls this "sin."

You can hate the word and try to rebrand it - but you can hardly deny the reality it affirms. Even if, for argument's sake, you take God out of the equation, nobody could honestly claim that they always thought, said or did what met with even *their own* standards of what is right. Let me test that. Would you, reading this now, be absolutely comfortable with the prospect, if it were possible, of having your every thought, word and deed -even in the last week- laid bare for all to see?

And we can't pretend that this powerlessness to live exactly as we know we should is just a local anomaly. It is a global pandemic. Everywhere you go in the world, on every continent and in every nation, at every time in history, you find exactly the same thing. There is not a human being on earth who is able to live a perfectly moral and upright life. Nor has there ever been before (except Jesus - and I will say more about his perfect life in chapter 12).

The consequences of sin are everywhere. It's so universal we take it for granted. We know it is not enough to have a front door for our houses; we need locks on them. We know it is not enough to have a lock on the car door; we need an alarm as well. We know it is not enough just to tell an official who we are. We need to provide proof of identity, and sometimes several different proofs. We know it is not enough to have a username for our e-mail accounts; we need passwords too, preferably different passwords for different accounts. And you'd better change them regularly as well. We know it is not enough for the Highways Agency to inform drivers of speed limits. They need radar and camera devices to enforce them.

We know it is not enough to have international borders. Nations have to defend them with military forces armed to the teeth.

Why? Because everyone knows that human nature, by itself, cannot be trusted. We are simply not virtuous. We are flawed – pretty well incurably. What the Bible calls "sin" is hardly an opinion - it's as near an established fact as any fact can be.

Incidentally, sin is hugely costly. Imagine all the resources that could be poured into feeding the hungry, educating the young, caring for the elderly and protecting the environment if we did not have to pay for defence, police, intelligence, security and prisons. But the biggest cost of sin, *far* greater and more serious than the economic one, is the chasm of separation, the alienation it opens up between people and God. Sin puts the human race in settled rebellion against God and his laws.

This is how the Bible puts it in Romans 3.10-12:

> *There is no one righteous, not even one;*
> *there is no one who understands;*
> *there is no one who seeks God.*
> *All have turned away,*
> *they have together become worthless;*
> *there is no one who does good, not even one.*

Then this conclusion shortly afterwards:

> *There is no difference between Jew and Gentile, [religious people and irreligious people] for all have sinned and fall short of the glory of God.*
>
> Romans 3.22-23.

American church leader Louie Giglio puts it very simply. He explains how easy God made it for people to be good by giving ten clear, basic and simple rules to live by; the Ten Commandments.

The first is not "You shall give all you own to the poor" or anything terribly demanding like that. The first commandment states; "You shall have no other gods before me." That's not hugely complicated. But when you try and find, anywhere on earth, anyone -*anyone*- who has never considered anything or anybody in their life more important to them than God you are bound to be disappointed. You will struggle to find a single soul.

Nobody, not even the most devout and saintly person on earth can even get past Number One of God's ten clear, basic and simple rules. This is what the Bible means when it affirms that all have sinned and have fallen short of God's standards.

It's a pessimistic assessment of who we really are. But it balances and complements the marvellous vision of being made in the image of God, declared "very good" by the Creator and loved by him (see chapters 5 and 6). The full biblical understanding of human nature is that we were all created glorious and unblemished but that we have all gone badly wrong.

As theologian Dr. Wayne Grudem explains, "It is not that some parts of us are sinful and others are pure. Rather, every part of our being is affected by sin – our intellect, our emotions and desires, our hearts (the centre of our desires and decision-making processes), our goals and motives, and even our physical bodies."[32]

The Reformers called this "total depravity" which sounds a bit overstated. But it does not mean that people can never do good things. That is demonstrably false. Clearly, people can. Rather it means that we are all indelibly tainted with a downward pull away from perfection and that we are totally unable to be right with God by our own efforts.

Of course, this whole approach is rejected by the secular humanist mind-set that is so dominant in the 21st Century Western world. This philosophy, in its vanity, tends to assume basic human goodness as a default position and even the word "sin" leaves secular commentators embarrassedly reaching for the Thesaurus for something a little more palatable.

> CS Lewis perceptively pointed out the inherent naivety in this approach in *Mere Christianity*. "It is only our bad temper that we put down to being tired or worried or hungry; we put our good temper down to ourselves."[33]

Funny, that. I have become self-satisfied and proud when I have acted in ways that are noble. And I have made excuses when I have acted in ways I regret. Haven't you? It's an experience as old as the Garden of Eden and as widespread as the human race is scattered.

We tend to take pride in our goodness - but it is an illusion that leads to spiritual emptiness and God seeming distant. We bury the guilt we feel about not being all we know we should be. When God shows us the truth about our self-righteousness and our need for Christ -and when we acknowledge both- everything falls into place.

Most people, if they are really honest, have a sense within them of never being as morally pure as they might be - and indeed *want* to be. But because in the Western world the Christian message is so marginalised in political circles and so misrepresented in the media, few understand what sin is and therefore few experience the wonderful release from its grip that Jesus offers.

When I became a Christian one warm July evening in 1979, I experienced three things; firstly, a sharp sense of my own sinfulness. I saw through all my pretending and posturing. I realised how shallow I was, how utterly unable I was to live a good life. The Bible calls this experience "the conviction of sin." I stopped living in denial and got real.

Secondly, I wept and wept over my wasted past, over all my vanity and self-importance. I wanted to be done with it, turn away from it and never go back. The Bible calls this "repentance."

Thirdly, I had a revelation of the love of God for me. Wave after wave of cleansing grace and favour poured into my soul. I knew I was loved. I knew I was a child of God. Oh, the joy of it! I knew I would never be the same again.

Over 30 years later, I still view my conversion as the most significant experience I have ever had. I catalogue everything in my life as before or after that event. And nothing, even falling in love, getting married and having children, has matched it for the intensity of its delight.

> *Happy are those*
> *whose transgressions are forgiven,*
> *whose sins are covered.*
> *Happy are those*
> *whose sin the Lord does not count against them*
> *and in whose spirit is no deceit.*
> Psalm 32.1-2.

That's the seventh reason why I am a Christian; sin is real. The evidence for it is everywhere. I'm as guilty of it as everyone else. But thank God, it is no longer counted against me - or anyone else who turns to him in repentance and faith.

Chapter 8

BEAUTY FROM UGLY THINGS

What good could come from your father committing suicide, from you stepfather abusing you, from your three daughters dying of cancer, from your family being murdered before your eyes and from ending up as a street kid in a foreign land? Read on...

In the last three chapters I have attempted to set out a basic biblical world view. But there's more to say. **What theologians call "providence" means that even life's worst tragedies are redeemable.** I've observed it so often that I have come to see it as consistent evidence of God at work in the world.

Are people like those whose circumstances I listed above just the victims of chance? Is it just bad luck? People who take this view think that there is no rhyme and reason to the way things happen, everything is meaningless, nothing is fair in the world and there's little you can do about it. Life is like Russian roulette. Or alternatively, are we at the mercy of fate? This view holds that the universe is manipulated and controlled in every detail. It's all written in the stars, everything is determined beforehand so your destiny is sealed and -again- there's little, if anything, you can do to change it.

Like one of those magic eye patterns where some people manage to discern a 3D image stepping out from a random, meaningless pattern, is providence a reality for those who have eyes to see?

Providence, unlike chance, says there *is* a rhyme and reason to the way things are because God wisely governs his universe, holding all things together. Life makes sense.

But providence, unlike fate, says there is something we can do about our future because God weaves our real choices into the narrative of his glorious plan.

The Bible verse that perhaps encapsulates best what providence is about is from Paul's letter to the Romans:

> *And we know that in all things God works for the good of those who love him, who have been called according to his purpose.*
>
> Romans 8.28.

Providence means that, if you are a Christian, everything works out in the end. Everything. That doesn't mean that God spares those who love him the worst things life could throw at them. Patently, that is not the case. Globally, Christians are among the worst treated people on earth (especially in parts of the Communist and Muslim worlds). No surprise there; Jesus said it would be so.[34]

But providence means that even life's greatest sorrows and disasters are redeemable. Something good can come from them and indeed the very greatest blessings often seem to be born from the deepest adversity and tragedy. I have seen it so many times that I have come to view it as evidence of God at work.

Providence means this: Almighty God, in his unrivalled sovereignty and immeasurable wisdom, sees to it that all circumstances, however dire, however adverse, however tragic, in the end work out for his glory and for the joy of a particular group of people; those who 1) love God and 2) are called according to his purpose. Oh, I love the doctrine of providence!

The tragedy is that for those who do not love God and who are therefore not called according to his purpose, suffering and tragedy are rarely productive. They tend much more to lead to bitterness, regret, despair and a hardening of the heart.

I have often noticed in pastoral work that personal grief, say the untimely death of a loved one or the birth of a severely disabled child, or a messy divorce, seems to either draw the people involved towards God or provoke a drifting away from faith – or worse, a bitter hatred of him.

One of Britain's most popular Christian songwriters, Matt Redman, has often spoken publicly of his experience of being told when he was 7 that his father had died, then learning two years later that the cause was suicide. He has also spoken about subsequently being abused as a teenager over a long period by his stepfather (for which he was convicted and jailed).

You can only imagine the confusion, pain, loneliness and self-doubt that those events would stir in a child's heart. But refusing a path of bitterness and choosing to turn to God in trust, Matt testifies to healing in his soul and how he has, by the grace of God, been able to break the cycle of grief and become a loving father in a wholesome family, even writing the tenderest songs about the Father heart of God.

A friend of mine from our time in France, Jacques Barbero, was for about 20 years a militant union leader in the steel industry. Jacques was a convinced atheist. Then tragedy struck. His three daughters, one after the other, contracted leukaemia. Jacques and his wife had the unspeakable sorrow of helplessly watching each of them fight a losing battle against their illness. They had to lay their three precious girls to rest before any of them reached adulthood. For many unbelievers, such a devastating grief would have surely hardened their atheism. How could a God of love have allowed such a thing?

But sometime after his season of distress, Jacques bumped into an Industrial Chaplain who explained that sickness and death are never God's perfect will for us. They come from living in a broken and fallen world. He urged Jacques to read the Bible.

Jacques' life was turned upside down. The consolation, the balm, the release he had so longed for - and had found nowhere else - flooded his soul. His life radically changed direction as the open wound of his sorrows found healing at last. Jacques started a charity called *Une Bible Par Foyer* (A Bible for Every Home) offering people God's word in marketplaces and street corners.

But most of all, this man who had been angry, militant, confrontational and anti-establishment became one of the gentlest, warmest, kindest and most peace-loving people I have ever known. He is also irrepressibly cheerful and positive. He has had a huge influence on everyone who knows him and he has a gift for bringing together deeply hostile factions so they work together in unity like no one I know.

Just today as I write this I was told about a man called William Sempija. William fled Rwanda after his parents and siblings were butchered before his eyes during the genocide. As a refugee he ended up as a street kid in Kampala in neighbouring Uganda. He lived ten years on the streets before he was spotted by a Christian and fostered. Miraculously, William began to achieve among the highest school grades in Uganda. After some time, William became a Christian and he now works with street children in Bwaise, Kampala. Over 250 children, orphans from war, AIDS or victims of poverty, are now cared for daily by his charity.

I am not saying that any of this makes the traumas suffered by Matt, Jacques, his wife and William as somehow OK. That's not what providence is about. The point I am making is that through providence, beautiful things can come from even life's worst tragedies. They needn't define our lives or condemn us to decades of resentment and regret.

Stories like these are legion in the Christian world and it is a running theme in Scripture too.

In Genesis 37-50, for example, there is the story of Joseph. An impulsive and gifted young man provokes the jealousy of his brothers who sell him into slavery. He ends up languishing in jail in Egypt after being falsely accused of sexual assault. Due to his gift of interpreting dreams he is brought before Pharaoh and made Vice President of Egypt. His rise to prominence averts mass starvation when a seven-year famine follows a seven-year period of plenty. The remarkable developments in the story show how he is eventually reconciled to his eleven brothers. The story ends when he reveals himself to them saying "You intended to harm me, but God intended it for good to accomplish what is now being done, the saving of many lives."

Then there is the story of Ruth. It's about a widowed young foreigner who shows amazing and sacrificial loyalty to her Israelite refugee mother-in-law (Naomi) when she could have pursued an opportunity to remarry while still young instead. The unexpected twists in the story show how it just so happened that everything worked out for good; Ruth eventually ended up harvesting in the field of a man named Boaz who just so happened to be distantly related to Naomi. And Boaz, under local laws and customs, it just so turned out had a moral obligation to consider marrying Ruth. The family tree growing from their marriage included David (Israel's greatest king) and their Messiah, Jesus.

What about the New Testament where, as Louie Giglio observes, all the good guys get killed? We know the Bible claims that it worked out well in the end for Jesus - raised on the third day. I'll say more about that in chapter 14. But what about John the Baptist (beheaded), Stephen (stoned), James (beheaded) and Peter (crucified upside-down)? What about Paul (imprisoned, severely flogged, exposed to death again and again, given the thirty-nine lashes five times, beaten with rods three times, pelted with stones, shipwrecked on three occasions, constantly in danger, deprived of sleep, often hungry and thirsty and eventually decapitated)?

Even then, their deaths resulted in an explosion of growth for the infant church. Persecution scattered Christians everywhere and the church rapidly spread. Tertullian, in his AD 197 work *Apologeticus* famously noted that the blood of the martyrs was the seed of the church. The more Christians were suppressed the more the message of Jesus got out and took root. That so many were willing to lay down their lives rather than deny their faith speaks of the strength of their conviction fuelled by witnessing the resurrection of Christ from the dead.

This is more than just ancient history though. These events illustrate the principle that tragedy, even death, never has the final word for those who love God and are called according to his plan.

In the mid 1990's I went through the worst period of my life. Kathie suffered three miscarriages in a little over a year and our children were being bullied and mugged at school. Our income was slashed making it hard to live on our budget. I was in a high-pressure/low reward job where I was being publicly undermined and forced out of work. Kathie was being stalked and threatened at her job in a local hospital for refusing to cover up a professional error. Our house was a building site - I could go on.

I would be lying if I were to say that my faith didn't wobble at all during that 3 year period. Pain and grief and discouragement and pressure seemed relentless and overwhelming. Doubts haunted me. Cynicism threatened to drag me down.

But I look back now and see that time as the most fertile ever period in my personal, emotional and spiritual development. I am so thankful for the character built in me over those years. I am grateful for the way it drove me to my knees – and so many prayers prayed through gritted teeth at that time have been answered over the long term. My family and I have truly prospered in every way.

> *We know that in all things God works for the good of those who love him, who have been called according to his purpose.*

I'll leave the last word to Malcolm Muggeridge. Born in 1903, he was an agnostic for most of his life, but he became a Christian at the age of 66 and wrote this in 1978:

> "Contrary to what might be expected, I look back on experiences that at the time seemed

especially desolating and painful, with particular satisfaction. Indeed, I can say with complete truthfulness that everything I have learned in my seventy-five years in this world, everything that has truly enhanced and enlightened my existence, has been through affliction and not through happiness, whether pursued or attained. In other words, if it ever were to be possible to eliminate affliction from our earthly existence by means of some drug or other medical mumbo jumbo . . . the result would not be to make life delectable, but to make it too banal or trivial to be endurable. This of course is what the cross [of Christ] signifies, and it is the cross more than anything else, that has called me inexorably to Christ."[35]

That's the eighth reason Christianity makes good sense to me; my experience of providence. Time and again I have observed that life's misfortunes do not have the last word for those who love God and who are called according to his plan.

Chapter 9

DON'T GO THERE

This chapter is of the book is atypical. It does not look at discoveries from the field of learning and say "How do you explain that then?" or look at something positive in Christian faith and say "I have found this to be real and true in my experience." All the others, with the exception perhaps of the last three, say "Look, this makes sense" or "Come on, taste and see that it's good."

But this chapter says, in effect, I am a Christian not just because I think the arguments for it are compelling or that my experience of it is satisfying, but also because the alternative to it is terrifying. I hesitated to include it because it might seem alarmist. But I can't deny that one of the reasons I hold to Christian faith is an entirely negative one: **Hell, if real, is portrayed by Jesus as an irrevocable eternity of anguished regret. That is not a risk I want to take.** Even if you don't think it's a big gamble because it seems to be from the world of fantasy, it cannot be denied that the price of being on the wrong side of the debate here is incalculable, however unlikely you think the prospect might be.

The fear of Hell used to be a significant factor in determining people's attitudes to Christianity in the UK. Certainly in the Middle Ages, the thought that you could spend an eternity in conscious torment was a highly effective deterrent against any kind of crime, but especially if it had a sacrilegious dimension. Until quite recently, for example, thieves might steal lead from the roofs of public buildings but to steal from a church was just considered to be beyond the pale. That was then. Now churches are not only fair game, they are actually singled out by thieves as easy targets. The Enlightenment challenged the authority of the Church and there has been a steady erosion of the fear of God in the Western World ever since. The idea that God is to be *feared* at all is now totally alien in our culture.

Subjects like God's judgment and Hell are rarely brought up in evangelistic conversation - it's as if doing so will end any remaining hope that the enquiring person might embrace the Christian message. But it's not just in conversation with seekers that Christians are noticeably silent on these things. God's judgment and Hell are virtually redundant as sermon topics in all but a few stalwart churches. It's as if mainstream Christianity is mortally embarrassed about any kind of final reckoning let alone divine sanction for wrongdoing.

On a superficial level you can see the erosion of the fear of God in the way our language has changed over the years. Chocolates that are particularly sweet are marketed as 'sinful'. An especially exhilarating theme park ride is "wicked." And "Hell" is actually a brand of sugar and caffeine-rich energy drink these days. What once made people shudder is now little more than an instant pick-me-up.

The images of Hell in the Bible are all thoroughly negative though. Not one word in the Bible suggests that it might be a place of alcohol-fuelled partying while the pious are subjected to the monotony of harp music on the clouds above. The word "Hell" is found 23 times in the New Testament: 12 times from the Greek *gehenna*, which means "place of burning," 10 times from the Greek *hades* which means "grave," and once from the Greek *tartarus*, which means "place of darkness."

Jesus, from whom we have more information on Hell than any other character in the whole Bible, described it as a frightening place of outer darkness where the noise of weeping and teeth gnashing are heard (Matthew 25.30) – that speaks of anguish and bitter regret. He talked about a place where worms never die and the fire is never extinguished (Mark 9.48) – that speaks of endless decay and destruction. In one of his parables, he talked about a man in Hell, begging for relief: "Cool my tongue, because I am in agony in this fire" (Luke 16:24). That speaks for itself. He said that Hell will be a place for the devil and his angels. (Matthew 25:41) – that doesn't sound like superb company. And he said "Do not be afraid of those who kill the body and after that can do no more… Fear him who, after your body has been killed, has authority to throw you into Hell." (Luke 12.4-5). So according to Jesus, the prospect of ending up there is literally a fate worse than death. There is a lot we don't know about Hell, but the verses above surely tell us all we need to know.

Why would Jesus talk about Hell so much and warn people about it so strongly if it were imaginary? If one thing is clear in the Gospels it's that Jesus *hated* hypocrisy and deplored deceitfulness. Knowingly misleading people about an imaginary punishment is appalling and runs completely contrary to Jesus' ethical standards.

When people ask me how I know Hell is real I answer, "I don't. But Jesus spoke about it as if it is. How do you know it *isn't*?" Why gamble with your soul?

Some people ask, "Is Hell just?" But is it just that all wickedness and corruption will never one day face justice? Is it just that people who have done unspeakably evil things and die peacefully in their beds will never one day have to give an account for their lives and be punished?

If you type *near death experience hell stories* into Google you'll find a host of testimonies from people, some formerly atheists, who claim to have had a foretaste of Hell when close to death. I don't know if any of these testimonies are worth reading. I tend to err on the side of scepticism and caution and I am not referencing any of them here. Look them up if you're interested and make your own mind up.

The thing is this; even if the chances of *just one* of these testimonies being true were 1 in 10 – or even 1 in 100, wouldn't it be foolish to dismiss it?

The veteran evangelist Billy Graham sometimes uses the analogy of getting on a plane. If you were told at an airport that the plane on the tarmac waiting for you to board had a 10% - or even 1% - chance of crashing would you get on it? Hell is infinitely worse than a plane crash.

Jesus' teaching (I'll say a lot more about that in chapter 12) is widely respected and hugely influential, even among those who do not call themselves Christians. It has authority. It cuts out all the waffle and is crystal clear. Its winsome wisdom has the ring of truth. What if the one who said inspiring things like "Love your enemies", "turn the other cheek and walk the second mile" and "let the one who is without sin throw the first stone..." what if he was equally inspired when he solemnly warned about the terrible reality of Hell?

Newcastle-based church leader David Holloway wrote recently, "Hell is self-chosen... No one can complain about the Bible's teaching on Hell. It is to stop you going there. It is a warning. It is like those danger signs on the cliff top and at electric pylons."[36]

Since discovering Jesus through my reading of the Gospels I have found him utterly convincing. Many years ago, I made the decision that I didn't want to get to the end of my life having ignored Jesus' warnings about Hell only to find it was true and too late, with no way back. It was not the prime reason for the change of direction in my life or even in the top ten. But it was definitely in the background.

The next five chapters will take us to the heart of why I think people should seriously consider the Christian faith – Jesus of Nazareth. If you were willing to read only two chapters of this book, I would want you to read Chapters 13 and 14.

But before the cross and resurrection it is recorded that Jesus spoke again and again about Hell as an irrevocable eternity of anguished regret. I think it's really unwise to hope that he was bluffing, or joking, or exaggerating, or misunderstood, or badly mistaken, or lying. What if, like everything else he said, he actually meant every word?

Chapter 10

WITH THE BENEFIT OF FORESIGHT

Who Jesus of Nazareth is and what he said and did are absolutely central to every Christian's identity.

The first thing to say about Jesus is that **his birth, life, death and resurrection were accurately predicted years before the events.** So many Old Testament prophecies about the Messiah are clearly fulfilled by him. I have yet to find anyone able to offer a satisfactory alternative explanation as to why they think Jesus of Nazareth is manifestly not the figure predicted in these texts.

Mathematician Peter W. Stoner, former Professor Emeritus of Mathematics and Astronomy at Pasadena City College, did some sums and calculated that the probability of just 8 such predictions being fulfilled in one person is one chance in one hundred million billion (which is many times more than the total number of people who've ever lived).[37]

Lee Strobel in *The Case for Christ* and Josh McDowell in *Evidence that Demands a Verdict* have made much of such data. They claim that there are hundreds of Old Testament prophecies about the expected Messiah and that Jesus fulfilled them all. Whilst I am sure their intentions are honourable, I have to say in the interests of fairness that I think these authors somewhat overstate their case though.

Some of the prophecies they reference are verses taken in isolation from longer passages that are not about the Messiah at all. Such verses only really apply to Jesus with imaginative hindsight (e.g. the famous verse about Emmanuel in Isaiah 7.1-17). By faith, I can of course see a prophetic dimension in such verses, reading back what I know from the Gospels. But because *sceptics* would not accept passages like these as legitimate evidence of prophetic fulfilment, I am not including those sorts of prophecies for consideration in this chapter.

Other prophecies were dramatically and self-consciously fulfilled by Jesus (e.g. the riding of a donkey on Palm Sunday as a deliberate fulfilment of Zechariah 9.9). Though, again, I personally accept these as legitimate fulfilments, because sceptics might dismiss them as being engineered by Jesus I am overlooking those kinds of prophecies here as well.

No matter. There are many other prophecies about the Messiah that do not fit either of the categories above. Considering *only these*, the case is still so evidentially strong and mathematically overwhelming that I consider it practically watertight.

Even limiting myself to a sceptic's measure of allowable evidence, it seems to me to be beyond reasonable doubt that Jesus' ancestry, birth, life, death and resurrection were precisely foretold centuries before the events happened.

Here are a few examples: in Genesis 12.3 we read that, of all human families, the whole earth will be blessed by a descendant of Abraham. In Genesis 17.19 we read that this promised bearer of blessing will be a descendant of Isaac, not Ishmael. In Genesis 49.10 we read that he will be from the tribe of Judah, not from any of the other 11 tribes of Jacob, or indeed from any of Esau's descendants. In Jeremiah 23.5-6 we read that he will be a descendant of David, not of any of Jesse's other seven sons or indeed from any other descendant of Judah at that time.

These four specific branches of the Messiah's family tree are all confirmed in Jesus' two independently compiled genealogies in Matthew's and Luke's Gospels. It is clear that they are independent because they differ at various points. (As an aside, though some point this out as evidence of factual error in the Bible, the two accounts are in fact consistent; Matthew traces Jesus' *legal* descent through his adoptive father Joseph, and Luke traces his *blood* descent through his natural mother Mary. Luke notes "He was the son, *so it was thought,* of Joseph").

Incidentally, no one can possibly now prove their ancestral lineage back to Abraham, Isaac, Jacob - or even to David - because all Jewish genealogical records were destroyed in the temple in 70 A.D., when the Romans razed Jerusalem to the ground, shortly after Matthew and Luke's Gospels were written down. Thus any new claim to be the fulfilment of Old Testament prophecy can never be verified – but Jesus' lineage has not one attesting source but two.

Then in Micah 5.2 it says that the Messiah will be born in Bethlehem, not Nazareth – or anywhere else for that matter. This detail is also corroborated in both Matthew's and Luke's Gospels. In Isaiah 61 it says that he will have a message of good news for the poor and will bind up the broken-hearted. This is a strong feature of his public ministry noted in all four Gospels.

At this point, sceptics may well allege that such details were woven in to the Gospel narratives by unscrupulous charlatans to make it *seem* that Jesus was the fulfilment of Old Testament prophecy when, in fact, he was nothing of the sort.

But is this really plausible? And where is the data supporting such claims? The evidence is, in fact, heavily stacked against such a theory.

Bear in mind that the origins of the Christian movement were highly explosive and that the expansion of the early Church sparked prolonged and violent opposition from both religious authorities and political rulers in the first century. Yet there is no hint anywhere of any challenge to the claims in the Gospels about Jesus' ancestry or birthplace. It would have been relatively easy for a contemporary of Matthew or Luke to suppress the early growth of Christianity with an evidence-based counterclaim that, for example, he was actually born in Nazareth, not Bethlehem and was from the tribe of Gad, not Judah. But there is not a trace of any controversy on this question.

On the contrary. The unmistakable fulfilment of Old Testament prophecy by Jesus was, as Martin Ayers perceptively notes, "a key factor in so many Jewish people becoming followers of Jesus. They had been waiting for the Christ, and in Jesus they found a man who ticked every box."[38] There is no chance that Jesus would have generated a significant following as Messiah amongst Jews unless his prophetic credentials were beyond doubt.

In any case, the early Christian movement was characterised by high standards of moral conviction where its adherents would not compromise an inch - even if the clear consequence was being torn apart by wild beasts in the Coliseum. If anyone can make a convincing case why so many would bravely accept being eaten alive just to prop up a motley collection of known exaggerations, half-truths, demonstrable factual errors and deliberate deceptions I have yet to hear it.

But the really heavyweight prophetic fulfilments concern not Jesus' origins, birth and life, but his death and resurrection.

Psalm 22 for example is a breath-taking prophetic prediction of the Messiah's sufferings. It tells of a man in extreme agony, thirsty, scorned and despised, the subject of derision ("let God save him if he trusts in him!"), his clothes gambled for and his hands and feet pierced. This Psalm, written by King David about 1,000 B.C., but patently not about himself, is particularly remarkable because the Jewish form of capital punishment was by stoning. Here, crucifixion is clearly in view ("they have pierced my hands and my feet"). But this was a form of execution devised and developed by the Romans about four centuries *after* Psalm 22 was written. In fact, in the days of King David, Rome itself hadn't even been founded!

Even more stunning is Isaiah 53, written about 750 B.C. (some scholars date it 200 years later but in any case it is comfortably earlier than half a millennium before Christ). It describes a figure who will be rejected by his own people, unjustly condemned without a whimper of protest, horribly disfigured by his beatings, pierced by his killers (for whom he will intercede), die from his injuries, be executed with wrongdoers but buried with the rich and, after death, see the light of life again and be satisfied.

The sharpness of focus in this picture of Christ's trial, flogging, crucifixion, burial arrangements and resurrection is absolutely awe-inspiring. And ten times in that one chapter Isaiah says that this figure, his suffering servant, will somehow take upon himself all the sorrows, sickness and sinfulness of fallen humanity - and pay for them, bringing healing and salvation to the guilty through his sufferings.

When the Dead Sea Scrolls were discovered in 1946, they found complete manuscripts of all the above mentioned prophecies. Through radiocarbon analysis it was established that the key Old Testament manuscripts, notably Isaiah, dated back to much earlier than 100 B.C. So there is no question of first century tampering with ancient texts to incorporate details of Jesus' life and death – just in case you were wondering.

I stated above that I think that writers like Josh McDowell and Lee Strobel, though I do not doubt their integrity, rather overegg the pudding. I stand by that. Nevertheless, even limiting ourselves to the prophecies above, and there are more, the statistical probability that Jesus is the realisation of Old Testament prophecy points to something approaching mathematical certainty.

Why is it that popular culture makes such a big deal out of obscure soothsayers like Nostradamus and prints vague horoscopes in every tabloid paper, yet fails to take any notice of convincing prophecy like this which, if true, is of supreme importance? Can anything be more perverse?

There's quite a lot I want to say about Jesus in the next four chapters; his persona is absolutely compelling, his teaching is uniquely appealing, his death solves emphatically the problem of sin (see chapter 7) and the evidence for his resurrection has won over the most adamant detractors - when they have bothered to look into it.

No one has had a greater impact on the course of world history than Jesus. I, along with billions of other Christians past and present, experience his presence and power in my life today. It all starts here with his faultless track record of perfectly fulfilling every messianic prophecy in the book.

Chapter 11

THE ONE AND ONLY

So Jesus clearly fulfilled many Old Testament prophecies but what sort of person was he? By common -almost universal- consent, **Jesus' persona is utterly amazing. Without ever being flashy, loud or gimmicky there is something undeniably compelling about Jesus.**

As one anonymous observer has noted, Jesus, by the sheer force of his persona, always defies the odds: "The greatest man in history is Jesus. He had no servants, yet they called him Master. He had no degree, yet they called him Teacher. He had no medicines, yet they called him Healer. He had no army, yet kings feared him. He won no military battles, yet he conquered the world. He committed no crime, yet they crucified him. He was buried in a tomb, yet he lives today."

Just picking out a few incidental details from the four Gospels, it is clear to see how charismatic Jesus was when he walked the earth. It seems he only had to say

"Follow me" and fishermen dropped their nets and tax collectors deserted their booths at once. People would travel for miles and press into crowded buildings to get anywhere near him. Yet he would stop everything to give his undivided attention, for however long it took, to one poor soul down on his or her luck. Children absolutely loved him and he rebuked his minders when they tried to impede their access to him.

No one in all history has had a personality remotely like his. He stands alone, head and shoulders above the rest. It's just like Homer Simpson said, "The Bible is full of messed up people - except for this one guy."

As John Stott put it in *The Contemporary Christian*, "It would be hopelessly incongruous to refer to him as 'Jesus the Great,' comparable to Alexander the Great, Charles the Great, or Napoleon the Great. Jesus is not 'the Great,' he is the Only. He has no peers, no rivals and no successors."[39] When you take a good look at Jesus you quickly become disappointed by comparison with everyone else on the planet.

Jesus defies categorisation. What Myers-Briggs personality type would he be? Surely a man who was constantly surrounded by crowds would have to be an extravert. But wouldn't a man who went to a solitary place *all night* to pray be a natural introvert? On all four Myers-Briggs scales I've found that it is impossible to label him.

He is above political pigeonholing as well. In the parable of the talents there is strong criticism for the servant who hides his savings under the mattress instead of investing it in projects that give a return. So he was a consummate capitalist, surely. But he never owned property, in fact had no possessions of his own, scolded the rich and had a particular concern for the underprivileged. So he must have been a proper socialist.

All through the Gospels his guilelessness is unmistakable. There is no trace in Matthew, Mark, Luke or John of a Jesus with a hidden agenda or any secret motive for personal gain. At his trial nobody could get a single charge to stick. Even his judge and executioners knew he was innocent and stated publicly that he was blameless.

His wisdom is indisputable. Every attempt to trap him flopped spectacularly. His poise and natural authority in such situations are breath-taking. The episode in John 8.1-11 (the woman caught in adultery) is a classic example. The agility with which Jesus effortlessly turned an impossible snare for him into a devastating exposure of his opponents' shabby hypocrisy -without trivialising the seriousness of adultery- is sensational. His brilliant reply "Let the one who is without sin throw the first stone" is so stunning in its effectiveness, so satisfying in its justice, yet so simple in its logic. It is flawless.

There is so much more that could be said. Historian H. G. Wells was once asked: "What single individual has left the most permanent impression on the world?" Wells immediately said "Jesus of Nazareth. It is interesting and significant that an historian like myself, with no theological bias whatever, cannot portray the progress of humanity honestly without giving him foremost place."[40]

This is undoubtedly true – and all the more remarkable given that we only really have information on about three years of his adult life. Jesus wrote no books, commanded no army, ruled no nation, left no monument, owned nothing, lived rough, died young and was given a hurried, unceremonious burial in someone else's tomb.

But his influence on history is commensurate with his unique personality. Of course it is the significance of his death and resurrection that account for his impact on history more than anything else and I shall come to that in chapters 13 and 14.

It is frankly depressing that so many people dismiss Christianity citing a few carefully selected misdemeanours or attitudes of some of its adherents as the reason. "What about the crusades?" "What about the Spanish Inquisition?" "What about all those wars that religion is responsible for? (Charles Phillips and Alan Axelrod in their exhaustive three-volume *Encyclopedia of Wars* estimate that just 7% of wars are religious in nature by the way).[41]

"What about all the church's preposterous wealth when millions are starving?" "What about paedophile priests?" "What about those hateful fundamentalists in the USA who picket military funerals?"

No matter that in each case those people brazenly ignore Jesus' teaching which specifically prohibits violence (Matthew 26.52), rejects the love of money (Matthew 6.24), demands a bias to the poor (Luke 14.12-14), warns of serious consequences for those who harm children (Matthew 18.6) and calls for the love of one's enemies (Matthew 5.44).

To those who raise such objections I always want to say "Forget Christendom. Look at *Christ* and tell me what you find wrong with *him*."

Being a Christian is about following *him*. It seems to me not only foolish but unfair to judge a movement by the actions of those who violate the plain teaching of its founder and head. Never has a baby been so unjustly thrown out with the bath water.

There's quite a lot more I want to say about Jesus in the next three chapters; his teaching is unique, his death changes everything, and the evidence for his resurrection is surprisingly sound. And part of the reason I have put my trust in Jesus and want to be like him is that the unequalled gravitas and attractiveness of his personality adds real weight to his perfect fulfilment of messianic prophecy.

But I want to end this chapter by quoting from the oratory of a gravel-voiced, old-time African-American Baptist preacher and civil rights activist called S. M. Lockridge (1913-2000). Lockridge once came up with the following magnificent word picture of Jesus.[42] When I say that Jesus' persona is absolutely compelling, this is what I have in mind:

> *He's the King of the Jews. He's the King of Israel. He's the King of righteousness. He's the King of the ages. He's the King of Heaven. He's the King of glory. He's the King of kings and He is the Lord of lords.*
>
> *No means of measure can define His limitless love. No far-seeing telescope can bring into visibility the coastline of His shoreless supplies. No barrier can hinder Him from pouring out His blessings.*
>
> *He's enduringly strong. He's entirely sincere. He's eternally steadfast. He's immortally graceful. He's imperially powerful. He's impartially merciful.*
>
> *He's God's Son. He's the sinner's saviour. He's the centrepiece of civilization. He stands alone in Himself. He's august. He's unique. He's unparalleled. He's unprecedented. He's supreme. He's pre-eminent.*

He's the loftiest idea in literature. He's the highest personality in philosophy. He's the supreme problem in higher criticism. He's the fundamental doctrine of true theology. He's the cardinal necessity of spiritual religion.

He's the miracle of the age. He's the superlative of everything good that you choose to call Him. He's the only one able to supply all of our needs simultaneously. He supplies strength for the weak. He's available for the tempted and the tried. He sympathizes and He saves. He's guards and he guides.

He heals the sick. He cleanses the lepers. He forgives sinners. He discharges debtors. He delivers the captives. He defends the feeble. He blesses the young. He serves the unfortunate. He regards the aged. He rewards the diligent and He beautifies the meek.

Well, my King is the key of knowledge. He's the wellspring of wisdom. He's the doorway of deliverance. He's the pathway of peace. He's the roadway of righteousness. He's the highway of holiness. He's the gateway of glory.

He's the master of the mighty. He's the captain of the conquerors. He's the head of the heroes. He's the leader of the legislators. He's the overseer of the overcomers. He's the governor of governors. He's the prince of princes. He's the King of kings and He's the Lord of lords.

His office is manifold. His promise is sure. His life is matchless. His goodness is limitless. His mercy is everlasting. His love never changes. His word is enough. His grace is sufficient. His reign is righteous. His yoke is easy and His burden is light.

I'm trying to tell you that the heaven of heavens can't contain Him, let alone a man explain Him... You can't outlive Him and you can't live without Him.

The Pharisees couldn't stand Him, but they found out they couldn't stop Him. Pilate couldn't find any fault in Him. The witnesses couldn't get their testimonies to agree. Herod couldn't kill Him. Death couldn't handle Him and the grave couldn't hold Him.

He always has been and He always will be. He had no predecessor and He'll have no successor. There's nobody before Him and there'll be nobody after Him. You can't impeach Him and He's not going to resign.

Thine is the kingdom and the power and the glory. Forever... and ever... and ever... And when you get through with all of the forevers, then Amen!

That's the incomparable Jesus I follow and love.

Chapter 12

NOW YOU'RE TALKING

In this chapter I want to take a look at the things Jesus said. I think **Jesus' teaching is supremely authoritative and uniquely appealing.**

Throughout the Gospels there are several recorded types of response to his words. Some people were offended, even outraged, such as the religious right 'moral majority' party then called the Pharisees.

Some were rendered speechless, notably the theologically liberal party called the Sadducees. These self-important intellectuals were the rationalist sceptics of Jesus' day but he exposed the incoherence of their supposedly superior ideas in ways that left them open-mouthed.

When put on the spot by the Jeremy Paxman and John Humphreys types of his day he left them reeling. So good were his answers and so perfect were they at exposing their hidden agendas that we are told on several occasions that nobody *dared* ask him any more questions.

Others were intrigued like, for example, Herod and Pilate - the authorities who were in charge of his trial. Still others were evidently perplexed particularly his rather slow-witted disciples.

But most people who listened to what he said seemed deeply impacted by his teaching. The most common recorded response was of wonder and admiration. In its day, Jesus' teaching was ground-breaking. It was fresh. It challenged the status quo. It exposed vested interests. It upset traditions. Jesus' teaching was, and remains, hardcore and radical. But we have got used to it now. Our culture has been shaped by much of what Jesus said so we don't always feel its impact the same way as those who first heard it did.

But do you know how it feels when you hear something new and eye-opening that has the ring of truth to it, that makes sense like nothing else you've ever heard, that causes wonderment and stirs in you the conviction that nothing will be the same again? Well, when Jesus opened his mouth to speak it was like that.

It is recorded that people responded to his words with amazement "because he taught them as one who had authority, not as the teachers of the law." "What is this?"

they asked. "A new teaching – and with authority!" (Mark 1.22 and 27). "Authority" means it was direct. It had clout. It addressed the things that mattered to ordinary people. It was in plain language. And it had *substance* (not like a politician's vague waffle about freedom, fairness and hardworking people who want to get on).

In Mark 12.37 it is recorded that the common people (literally the *hoi polloi*[43]) listened to him with delight. His words had the emotional effect of lifting the mood and giving inspiration with something genuinely new.

There is a slightly comical passage in John's Gospel (John 7.45-46) where the establishment dispatch a few temple guards to locate Jesus, get hold of him and bring him back for a ticking-off. The henchmen sit engrossed listening to him and return empty handed. The chief priests, exasperated, demand to know where he is. "But no one ever spoke the way this man does!" they report, open mouthed.

In contrast to our self-promoting celebrities, our hyped-up athletes, our evasive politicians and our platitudinous vicars (examples of each readily spring to mind and, yes, I hold up my hand) *nobody* ever reacted to what Jesus said with yawning indifference. Absolutely no one. And even twenty centuries later, the wisdom of Jesus' teaching is still matchless, its clarity is peerless and its moral goodness is timeless. You don't get to be the most quoted person in history for mouthing platitudes, inanities and muddled opinions.

I have sometimes wondered what kind of world we would live in if everybody in this world obeyed Jesus' teaching – or even *tried* to. There would be no wars. There would be instant and lasting resolution to even the most protracted and insoluble conflicts. Able people would be slow to judge those less gifted. Everyone would learn to be content with what they had and never worry about a thing. Crime rates would nosedive. Those who were victims of accidents would be quick to forgive. Everyone would be insanely generous. Leaders would be unmoved by prestige. Political office would be untainted by corruption, sleaze, abuse of power and everything else we seem to get fed up about every five or ten years.

But I digress… Jesus' teaching is *so* good that Christians have rarely had to defend Jesus' words against a global tsunami of indignation; far from it.

The Philosopher John Stuart Mill (1806-1873) for example, who was not a Christian, said this in his *Essay on Theism*: "About the life and sayings of Jesus there is a stamp of personal originality combined with profundity of insight which… must place the prophet of Nazareth, even in the estimation of those who have no belief in his inspiration, in the very first rank of men of sublime genius of whom our species can boast."[44]

Even Christianity's most vociferous opponents have had to recognise the imperious excellence of Jesus' teaching and not just through gritted teeth either. Richard Dawkins -yes, even him- so admires the Sermon on the Mount that he once had a t-shirt made with the slogan *Atheists for Jesus*. He rather reverts to type though by rather laughably claiming that Jesus would be an atheist if he were around today.

But we can't have Jesus on our own terms. He is not ours to claim as a figurehead of our interest group, whatever it might be, religious or otherwise.

It is intellectually dishonest to pick out, for example: "love your enemies," "don't parade your righteousness before others," "go the second mile," "blessed are the merciful for they will be shown mercy" and "why do you point out the speck in someone's eye when you have a plank in your own eye?" as if they were dreamed up as humanist axioms.

All those phrases come from the same block of Jesus' teaching which contains 20 references to God or "your heavenly Father," includes an endorsement of the Old Testament, a warning about Hell, instruction on prayer, and a call to live with the perspective of eternity in Heaven.

However much humanists might approve of Jesus' enlightened and enlightening words, his basic message is about the kingdom of *God*, not the supremacy of man.

This expression "the kingdom of God," comes over 80 times in his teaching and is the theme of over two thirds of his parables; stories simple enough for young children to understand and enjoy but subtly layered enough for grown adults to scratch their heads in stunned bewilderment.

His words were also uncompromisingly challenging. How's this for a rallying call to join a movement?

> *Whoever wants to be my disciple must deny themselves and take up their cross daily and follow me. For whoever wants to save their life will lose it, but whoever loses their life for me will save it. What good is it for someone to gain the whole world, and yet lose or forfeit their very self?*
>
> Luke 9.23-25.

To a wealthy young man who wanted to join the movement Jesus said, "All right. First, sell all you have and give to the poor. Then follow me." When he turned away because he wasn't quite willing to go *that* far Jesus didn't stop him in his tracks and call out "O.K., Maybe 50% then." He just let him go and used the encounter to teach those around. "How hard it is for the rich to enter the kingdom of God!" And just in case they still weren't sure he added: "No one who puts a hand to the plough and looks back is fit for service in the kingdom of God." Not for wimps then. Jesus commands -and deserves- total, not token, commitment. His is a cause worth living and dying for.

Perhaps the most surprising element of Jesus' teaching, especially for one so celebrated for his humility, is his self-revelation. Anyone who speaks about him- or herself in the third person is either embarrassingly conceited or, much more rarely, the real deal. Jesus said an awful lot about who he was; he gave himself titles, he called people to follow him, to believe in him, to give up everything for him. He explained who he was in relation to God the Father, he often explained why he had come and he repeatedly predicted his death and rising again.

Imagine *anyone* you know calling themselves "the (not *a* but *the*) Good Shepherd," saying "if you've seen me, you've actually seen God," challenging others to leave everything they have to follow them and explaining that they came into the world to seek and save sinners. It would be preposterous. They'd be *locked up*. Or sent down for fraud.

Well, maybe Jesus *was* a mental case. He'd have to be seriously unhinged if he mistakenly thought he was the Light of the World who is one with God the Father. Or maybe he was the calculating and charismatic leader of a false cult. That would make Christianity *easily* the biggest fraud ever pulled off in human history. For me though, all four Gospels are strikingly consistent. Jesus' matchless teaching, his inspiring persona and the passionate and loyal following he attracted all add up to one conclusion; he's the real deal.

I have come to reflect on Jesus' teaching over the last 30 years or so and I find that it eloquently supports the truthfulness of Christianity. But I didn't become a Christian in a cool and calculated cerebral response to having worked it all out in my mind. Not at all.

It started with a surprising spiritual encounter and a profound emotional experience. First of all, I *felt* my way to being a Christian. It was an encounter much more of the heart than of the mind. Only afterwards did I look into it all and try to make sense of what happened to me. When I did, I found that everything I looked into confirmed and gave meaning to my experience. And nothing more so than the cross of Christ – which is what the next chapter is about.

Chapter 13

THE CRUX OF THE MATTER

So Jesus fulfilled Old Testament prophecy, and lived like and talked like no one else who has ever lived, but **it's Jesus' death that changes history forever by resolving the problem of sin.**

The symbol of Christianity is not a manger or any feature of Jesus' itinerant ministry; it's a cross. For Christians, the central feature of Jesus' time on earth is not his unusual birth, or his revolutionary teaching, or even his amazing miracles; it's his ignominious death. And for Christians, Jesus' death is of more than mere personal interest -it's bigger than just 'saving my soul so I can go to Heaven'- it is the very fulcrum of human history.

At one level, you could say there is nothing remarkable at all about Jesus' death. Roman occupied Judea in the first century saw dozens of young Jewish revolutionaries making a bit of a stir, exciting a popular following and ending up on a cross when they unsettled the *pax romana* a bit too much for the governor's liking. To the Romans, Jesus was just another would-be messiah who was ruthlessly silenced for disturbing the peace. All these popular messiah movements subsided immediately following their hero's demise and nothing more was heard of them. This one would no doubt follow the same script.

But of course, the events surrounding Jesus' last 24 hours are quite unique. Caesar didn't quite get what he bargained for this time. Why has the judicial murder of Jesus of Nazareth become by far the best known tribunal and execution in human history?

Why is it that the popular following centred on this Galilean carpenter-turned-preacher is the only one that did not collapse and fade into obscurity on the death of its leader; in fact, quite the reverse? Why did it explode into life and conquer the ancient world - and in the face of severe persecution moreover? Mostly, that was to do with the resurrection which we'll come to in the next chapter. But, even putting that to one side for a moment, Jesus' death itself has immense significance. The resurrection would not at all mean the same thing if Jesus had just died of some illness or of old age.

Much ink has been spilled on the subject of who should shoulder the blame for Jesus' death. The Gospels show that no one comes out of the narrative particularly well.

The Jewish leaders were guilty of pursuing Jesus to death because he was such a threat to their religion and their positions of power. The Roman procurator Pontius Pilate was guilty of condemning him, knowing full well he was innocent. The Roman military was guilty of acting with excessive, sadistic cruelty when its soldiers met no resistance from the condemned man in their charge. Judas was guilty of betraying Jesus for a bag of coins and the other disciples were guilty of deserting him and denying knowledge of him having sworn just hours earlier that they never would. But the matter of finding a scapegoat for Jesus' death is of no real interest to the Gospel writers - and we should not be distracted by it either.

The Gospels are much more interested in stressing Christ's innocence than finding someone to blame. And Jesus' innocence was beyond doubt. Not a single charge stuck. No two witnesses were consistent. Not a shred of damning evidence for any crime was produced. Nothing in cross examination added up. Pontius Pilate would have been delighted to have been able to find Jesus guilty of something - anything; it would have kept the excitable rabble outside his palace quiet. He could have gone to bed and been done with it. But, the closer Pilate examined the case, the more persuaded he became that Jesus was being framed. In all four Gospels, Pilate attempts to reason with those baying for his blood. Wary of getting drawn into an internal Jewish squabble he doubtless had little appetite for, he tries on four occasions to avoid sentencing Jesus.

At first, he just declares the case closed, finding the charges frivolous and a waste of his time. When that doesn't wash, he tries to pass the buck to Herod who happens to be in town for the Passover. Let him sort his squabbling fanatics out. But Jesus doesn't cooperate at all, completely blanking the vain, self-important fool who had stupidly executed his cousin John the Baptist. When that doesn't work, Pilate tries to bargain with those intent on doing away with Jesus, offering the obviously unpalatable option of releasing a violent insurgent onto the streets instead. When even that backfires, he has Jesus beaten to within an inch of his life, hoping the Chief Priest and his cronies will agree that it's enough to make Jesus go away quietly. No chance. Only when the mob blackmails Pilate with the threat of reporting him to Caesar for weakness and disloyalty does he give up and sign the death warrant they demand.

Never has anyone been so manifestly innocent. And yet never has a miscarriage of justice been so inevitable. No ingenious scheming or herculean effort could have stemmed this inexorable tide of events. It wasn't an accident. Jesus *had* to go to the cross. Nothing could have stopped it. It was God's sovereign resolve to proceed with the unthinkable. This is why he came.

Pathological studies of crucifixion make upsetting reading. The positioning of a man's body on a cross made it difficult to breathe. The Victorian author and Fellow at Cambridge University Frederic Farrar described this graphically in his book *The Life of Christ*:

> "A death by crucifixion seems to include dizziness, cramp, thirst, starvation, sleeplessness, traumatic fever, tetanus, shame, publicity of shame, long continuance of torment, horror of anticipation, mortification of untended wounds, all intensified just up to the point at which they can be endured at all, but all stopping just short of the point which would give to the suffer the relief of unconsciousness."[45]

According to the prominent expert in forensic pathology Dr. Frederick Zugibe, the piercing of the median nerve of the hands with a nail can cause pain so incredible that even morphine is of little use, "severe, excruciating, burning pain, like electric shocks traversing the arm into the spinal cord." Rupturing the foot's plantar nerve with a nail would have a similarly unpleasant effect.

Such is the uniqueness of the pain and distress of suffering crucifixion, that the English language accommodated a new word in its vocabulary to adequately express that agony. We call unbearable suffering "excruciating" – *ex* meaning "from" or "out of" and *crux* or *cruci* meaning "cross." Excruciating means "out of the cross."

Dr. Zugibe concluded that Christ probably died from heavy loss of blood and fluid, plus traumatic shock from his injuries, plus cardiogenic shock, causing Christ's heart to pump weakly, then fail altogether.[46]

But interestingly, there are no details whatsoever about what the crucifixion actually looked like in the Gospels. They don't say, "There was so much blood…" or anything of that sort. There is no description of his physical suffering at all. Nor is there the slightest speculation among the Gospel writers about what Jesus may have died from. Was it cardiac rupture, shock, asphyxiation, dehydration? That may be our interest, but it wasn't theirs. The New Testament doesn't tell you what it was like; it tells you what it *means*.

All those Old Testament sacrifices, so laboriously prescribed, all that shedding of blood (to show that sin is deadly serious), all that offering your very best lamb (to make the point that forgiveness is not cheap) looked towards this moment. All those obscure prophecies in the Old Testament about a suffering -yet triumphant- Messiah come into focus here. Like an unexpected twist in the last chapter of a great novel in which the seemingly incidental subplots all find satisfactory resolution, the cross makes sense of everything.

In chapter 7 I argued that sin offers the best explanation there is of what's wrong with the world. It deforms us. It leads to untold misery. It estranges us from God. It messes up all relationships. It fractures our vision of all that is good and true. It spoils everything. That is the Christian explanation for why there is so much misery on earth.

And the Christian vision of how all that can be reversed and healed is the cross of Christ. This is the one and only way to right the wrong of sin. Through the cross we can be reshaped, we can be reconciled to God, we can enjoy truly wholesome relationships, we begin to see goodness and truth the right way up and our eyes become opened to anticipate the renewal of all things.

Perhaps the best known verse in the Bible, John 3.16, says:

> *God so loved the world that he gave his one and only Son, that whoever believes in him shall not perish but have eternal life.*

The cross means this: because God loves us, he didn't just leave us just to make a mess of our lives and assume the consequences. He came to sort it all out.

Sometimes people misunderstand the New Testament message and suggest that God is in some way unfair. "How can God punish an innocent man on behalf of other people? That's unjust and immoral." Some have even called it "cosmic child abuse" and condemned it as sadistic or sick.

But that is a gross misunderstanding and misrepresentation of the atonement. The point is -as the Bible specifically claims- that "God was in Christ, reconciling the world to himself." God himself came in the person of his Son Jesus Christ, to die in our place and to make it possible for us to be forgiven and restored.

And anyway Jesus was not an unwilling victim. "No one takes my life from me" he said, "I lay it down of my own accord" (John 10.18).

Amazing love! There is nothing that lights up my life more brightly than an insight into the sheer majesty and wonder of the cross. It's like a brilliant shaft of sunlight that suddenly breaks through heavy blanket cloud on a grey afternoon. The experience of knowing myself to be -and truly feeling- cleansed, loved and forgiven is sheer delight. It is health to my soul. Nothing compares.

So Jesus' bursting onto the scene in about 30 A.D. wasn't just another of those failed uprisings, here today, gone tomorrow, squashed by the ruthless might of Rome. No. Jesus' death, grimly unexceptional in its day, became world history's best known trial and execution for a very good reason.

Not least because this particular Messiah movement remains to this day the only one that provoked a massive public disturbance about the body of the executed man going missing three days later. Some even said they'd seen him alive again and nothing, not even the threat, and meting out, of violence could silence them.

And that's when this small, defeated, ragbag collection of lame ducks and small town losers became an unstoppable force all over the then-known world, growing faster than the Empire could strike back and throw them to the lions. "He is alive and has appeared to us" they claimed. Many thought they were completely mad and dismissed them as an eccentric irrelevance. But those who embraced the movement found the force within it changed their lives beyond their wildest dreams.

And that's the next chapter is about.

Chapter 14

RISE AND SHINE

I have already looked at Jesus' atoning death, his compelling persona, his remarkable fulfilment of Old Testament prophecy and his unique teaching. But this one is the most crucial of all. **Evidence for Christ's resurrection is amazingly sound and stands up to serious cross-examination.**

New York City based author Tim Keller rightly argues that Christianity stands or falls on one thing alone.

"If Jesus rose from the dead, then you have to accept all that he said; if he didn't rise from the dead, then why worry about any of what he said? The issue on which everything hangs is not whether or not you like his teaching but whether or not he rose from the dead."[47]

I absolutely agree. Either Christianity is supremely central to life (if the resurrection really happened) or it is irrelevant and even contemptible (if it didn't).

The Apostle Paul made the same point about 15-20 years after Jesus' death. Here's a modern paraphrase of what he said:

> *If there's no resurrection for Christ, everything we've told you is smoke and mirrors, and everything you've staked your life on is smoke and mirrors. Not only that, but we would be guilty of telling a string of barefaced lies about God, all these affidavits we passed on to you verifying that God raised up Christ—sheer fabrications, if there's no resurrection. If corpses can't be raised, then Christ wasn't, because he was indeed dead. And if Christ weren't raised, then all you're doing is wandering about in the dark, as lost as ever. It's even worse for those who died hoping in Christ and resurrection, because they're already in their graves. If all we get out of Christ is a little inspiration for a few short years, we're a pretty sorry lot.*
> 1 Corinthians 15.14-18 - The Message.

In other words, without the resurrection Christianity is false, Christian belief is futile, the Bible is fake and death is final.

Like Achilles' heel, if you can successfully attack and disprove the resurrection, you fatally undermine Christianity, consigning it lock, stock and barrel to the dustbin of history. Given the fantastic opportunity anti-theists have of discrediting Christianity and removing it from the list of world religions by proving the resurrection to be false, it is remarkable that so few of them have seriously attempted to do so.

Some have though. About 260 years ago, two atheist lawyers from Oxford named George Lyttelton and Gilbert West decided to disprove the Christian faith by each writing a book.

Lyttelton set out to demonstrate that the conversion of Saul of Tarsus (the Apostle Paul) was a myth and West determined to debunk the resurrection of Jesus from the dead. Each spent a full twelve months in painstaking research to establish his case. When they had completed their studies they met up to compare notes. Lyttelton confessed "As I have studied the evidence from a legal standpoint, I have become convinced that Saul of Tarsus *was* converted just the way described in Acts." And West, having sifted the evidence for the resurrection most carefully and painstakingly, became satisfied that Jesus almost certainly did rise from the dead at the first Easter just as the Gospels claim. So exhaustive and scholarly was West's work that the University of Oxford awarded him a higher doctorate for it. Both men became Christians in the course of their research.

West's rather laboriously titled book *Observations on the History and Evidences of the Resurrection of Jesus Christ* printed a quotation on the flyleaf:

Do not find fault before you investigate.
                                    Ecclesiastes 11.7.

But sadly many people *do* find fault before they investigate. Many just say that the idea of a dead body coming back to life is simply ridiculous so therefore the resurrection must be categorised with fairies at the bottom of the garden, assertions that the earth is flat and sightings of Diana and Elvis playing golf on the moon.

As I mentioned in chapter 4, the irony of this viewpoint is that it is often held by the same people who also vigorously argue that non-living matter *did* become living matter all by itself many millions of years ago in the evolution of life on earth.

When sceptics actually take the trouble to look into the resurrection of course they usually refuse the writings of the New Testament as admissible evidence. Four reasons are usually given;

1) The Gospels were made up many years after the events.
2) They are inherently biased.
3) They fail to name any sources to substantiate their claims.
4) And in any case the four reports of the resurrection contain fatal contradictions.

For those four reasons, many people dismiss the Gospels as texts unworthy of a second look. But each objection encounters difficulties.

1) On the reliability of the Gospels, the best scholarship dates the earliest, Mark, at around 64-76 AD, perhaps as little as 30 years after Jesus' death. Because there are so many similarities between Matthew and Luke that are not contained in Mark, it is clear that they must have drawn on further common source material readily available at the time (scholars call this material "Q") so there is little doubt that the Gospels are substantially primitive accounts. For obvious reasons, the earlier an account is to the events it describes, the less likely it is to have been embellished or exaggerated along the way.

2) On the question of bias, the problem is that it wasn't only Jesus' band of brothers who propagated this news. Saul of Tarsus for example ruthlessly attempted to *suppress* and *extinguish* the resurrection rumours at first. It was only after a dramatic conversion experience that he became one its chief heralds. Jesus' brother James was another noted sceptic and cynic[48] until he witnessed the risen Christ and then became a leading figure in the church at Jerusalem.

3) On the question of the historicity of the Gospels, it is true that they fail to name sources but history was recorded differently in 1st Century Judea than it is in 21st century Europe. It is surely unfair to judge the literature of one age by the standards of another. Otherwise, shall we have to write Shakespeare off as illiterate because he rarely spelled his name the same way twice? There is enough variance in the four Gospels to establish that they clearly drew on different but complementary sources.

Furthermore, the eminent and scholarly archaeologist Sir William Mitchell Ramsay, after spending two decades researching the areas Luke wrote about, with the specific goal of discrediting the Acts of the Apostles as historically inaccurate, concluded that Luke's attention to detail was impeccable and that he made *no factual mistakes*. "You may press the words of Luke in a degree beyond any other historian's and they stand the keenest scrutiny and the hardest treatment" he wrote.[49]

4) The apparent contradictions (e.g. was it dark or light when the women set out and how many of them were there?) have been perceptively accounted for in books like *Easter Enigma* by Greek scholar John Wenham and *Who Moved the Stone* by journalist Albert Henry Ross, under the pseudonym of Frank Morison.

Wenham conducts a detailed and fascinating reconstruction of the movements of the chief characters which perfectly harmonises the four accounts.

Ross set out to forensically analyse all the material and write a book entitled *Jesus – the Last Phase* to show that the resurrection was an ancient myth. He ended up, like Gilbert West, changing his mind altogether and becoming a Christian. Confessing that he wanted to strip the last week of the life of Jesus "of its overgrowth of primitive beliefs and dogmatic superstitions" Ross had to change his plans.

"Things emerged from that old-world story which previously I should have thought impossible. Slowly but very definitely the conviction grew that the drama of those unforgettable weeks of human history was stranger and deeper than it seemed. It was the strangeness of many notable things in the story that held my interest. It was only later that the irresistible logic of their meaning came into view."[50]

The internal evidence (that which is found in the Bible) for the resurrection has been laid out many times by many people and I am not going to repeat it at length here. But briefly:

1) The resurrection of the suffering Messiah had been prophesied centuries before the birth of Jesus (see chapter 10).

2) On several occasions, Jesus had himself predicted his own resurrection while teaching his disciples – who didn't understand what he was saying until it actually happened.[51]

3) According to Matthew, Mark, Luke and John, the body had vanished from the tomb. But Luke and John also note that the burial shroud and head bandage were still in place. Why would any tomb raider steal the body, but leave the burial cloths in exactly the same place as they had been when they had covered the corpse?

4) If the Jewish authorities or Roman guards had removed the body, why did they not exhume it to put an end to the excited and increasingly troublesome proclamation - in that very same city and just six weeks later - that Jesus was alive?

5) If the disciples removed it and lied that they had not, why did they not back down or go away quietly when faced with physical violence, imprisonment and the death penalty?

6) And in any case, how would anyone have got past armed security guards at the tomb, shift the stone and remove the uncovered body completely unnoticed?

7) According to 1 Corinthians 15, many eyewitnesses, over 500 people "most of whom are still living", saw Jesus alive after his death. The challenge of the passage is "If you haven't seen him yourself, go and ask someone among hundreds who has."

8) If the Gospel reports of the resurrection were fabricated, why were women the first recorded witnesses of it? Their testimony was not admitted as reliable in the ancient world so there was nothing at all to be gained by noting that they witnessed the empty tomb and the risen Jesus before anyone else did. In the same way, if I wanted to concoct a story about seeing the Loch Ness Monster or a UFO, I would not help my chances of deceiving people if I choose young children or my own family as my principal witnesses because their testimony would be widely viewed as unreliable or suspicious. I would pick someone more believable.

The striking thing about the Gospel reports is that they are so incidental. They make no inferences and draw no conclusions. No one says "The burial cloth was still there so therefore that rules out grave robber hypothesis." There's no exaggeration either. No one says "OMG, it was mind-blowing, it was awesome!" as if they are selling you something. The Gospel writers are remarkable for their understatement. They just tell you the bare facts about what people remembered from that morning; nothing more, nothing less.

You can read much more about the internal evidence in books like the two I mentioned above. The excellent *Gunning for God* by John C. Lennox also has an outstanding and well researched chapter on this subject.

The external or circumstantial evidence is also very strong.

1) Why were the eleven surviving disciples, without exception, completely transformed individuals with the resurrection at the heart of their message? These people had fled, understandably fearing for their lives, when Jesus was arrested. What *happened* to them? Only something totally out of the ordinary accounts for such a dramatic and permanent change in their behaviour.

2) Why did the earliest Christians, who were all devout Jews, suddenly change their "holy day" from the Sabbath to the first day of the Jewish working week – Sunday? From having always worshiped on their weekly day of rest, the observance of which was regulated to near obsessive levels, they started to meet instead the following day at dawn before going to work. There would have to have been a momentous reason to make them turn their backs on centuries of deeply entrenched religious

practice. If Muslims began to gather for prayer on Saturday rather than Friday, or if Christians started to hold services on Monday before work rather than Sunday, we would rightly conclude that a seismic cultural shift had occurred and that something out of the ordinary would have to account for it.

3) How is it that a thoroughly laughable story, originating from a motley band of unpromising losers in a backwater province of imperial Rome, became what is still today the world's biggest movement? Christianity took on the might of the Roman Empire and, despite widespread contempt and brutal persecution, soon eclipsed it for cultural significance. How can we account for the improbable and meteoric rise of this deeply loathed and illegal sect?

One thing only can explain it – the resurrection of Christ from the dead. People everywhere began to believe it because they felt its life-changing aftershocks in their own personal experience. Millions all over the world still do. No, the more you look into the resurrection, the more it *adds up*. The more you try to come up with an alternative explanation, the more it looks like desperation.

I have emphasised evidence quite a lot up till now because I believe it is so sound. I know, I know. People these days don't tend to ask "is it true?" These days people want to know "does it work?" or even "how does it feel?"

But I'm not a Christian just because it gives me a warm glow inside. Christianity really, really matters because, above all else and no matter what you feel about it, it is *true*. And no matter how good it might feel, if it is untrue Christianity is of no consequence at all, it is the worst scam in world history and should be held in the highest contempt. I can't find any value in moderate Christianity if it is based on false testimony.

As CS Lewis once wrote in *God in the Dock*: "One must keep on pointing out that Christianity is a statement which, if false, is of no importance, and, if true, is of infinite importance. The one thing it cannot be is moderately important."[52]

But if you don't *want* to believe, no amount of evidence will be enough for you. However, if you want to believe, you can have an experience of Jesus that touches the deepest depths of your being. From chapter 17 onwards, I will emphasise experience more than logic.

For now though, the 14th reason I am a Christian is because I am convinced that Jesus rose from the dead. Nothing has persuaded me otherwise, and Christ's wonderful, life-giving, joy-filling presence in my life day after day brings my heart into glad agreement with my head.

Chapter 15

THE INVISIBLE EDITOR

In the next three chapters I am going to look at the Bible and why I think it is inspired like no other book.

Firstly, I am struck by what I see as its extraordinary unity and coherence. **The Bible's message is amazingly consistent with a striking running theme.**

As you read those words, I admit that they may not generate that much of a "wow" factor but when you think about it, they really should.

Think of it this way. Imagine someone asks you to select and assemble into one volume 66 assorted pieces of literature, covering a 1,500 year timespan, authored by legislators, historians, poets, farmers, royalty, manual workers, political commentators, songwriters, tax administrators and family doctors, written in three different languages and from the cultures of three different empires on three different continents. However hard you tried, it would be no great surprise if the fruit of your labours turned out to be a ragbag assortment of miscellaneous and often contradictory texts.

Now consider the Bible. It is a collection of 66 quite different writings, some quite long, some very short, in over a dozen distinct genres[53] written over one and a half millennia, by about 35-40 different authors, most of whom didn't know each other or consult together, from all the social backgrounds listed above and more besides, and immersed in cultures as disparate as the Egyptian (Africa), Babylonian (Asia) and Roman (Europe) empires. Not one of those authors knew they were contributing to the same anthology.

The result though is decidedly not the weird jumble of unconnected ideas you might reasonably expect from such widely diverse sources. In fact, though hundreds of themes are explored in the Bible from a bewildering array of viewpoints, and in many different styles, it speaks with one voice. I think that is humanly inexplicable.

If you are shaking your head in disagreement, let me give three examples of what I mean. 1) There is for example, from Genesis to Revelation, absolute agreement on the nature of God; his wisdom, his power, his truthfulness, his love, his holiness, his justice, his patience, his authority, and his consistent, principled hostility to sin that is called his wrath. Throughout the 66 books an intriguingly uniform picture of God emerges.

2) Furthermore, from beginning to end, there is also absolute agreement on the condition of humankind. Our species is consistently presented as lovingly created, superior in moral responsibility to all other animals, yet, -unlike them- inevitably sinful and flawed, and always dependent on God's grace to initiate and maintain any relationship with God.

3) And throughout Old and New Testament the reader is constantly reminded that there will be a Day of Final Reckoning when God will judge the world in perfect fairness. There is no hint of reincarnation, only resurrection in a restored creation.

That's just three examples. There are many more.

But the Bible does much more than just not disagree with itself if you'll excuse the awkward English. The Bible has, in addition, a profound coherence with a distinct sweeping narrative and clear central plot.

The overarching story in the Bible has been neatly summed up as the tale of three trees. Firstly, the Tree of the Knowledge of Good and Evil in Genesis 3 is the explanation, however literally or figuratively you read it, of how things got to be so messed up in our beautiful world. In theological terms, it's about how sin entered the world. Secondly, the cross on which Jesus was crucified, taking upon himself the penalty for sin, is referred to twice in the Acts of the Apostles literally as a *tree* (Acts 5.30 and Acts 10.39). This is the explanation of how God stepped in to repair everything. And thirdly, the Bible ends in Revelation 22 with a vision of a restored creation, centred round an evergreen, permanently fruitful, Tree of Life, whose leaves are for the healing of the nations.

Basically, the Bible is the story of a beautiful and perfect world that is ruined, then rescued and finally restored. That basic narrative is the golden thread that runs through every book in the Bible. Every subplot, however self-contained and interesting in its own right, contributes to and finds its deepest significance in that central theme.

It would take far too long to illustrate how this is so all the way through the Bible. But here are just four examples.

1) Right from the start in the story of The Fall, there is the promise that a male figure, the offspring of a woman, would come to crush the head of the serpent (Genesis 3:15). One day, the wrongs of the Garden of Eden would be righted. Then right at the end of the story, in the book of Revelation, Jesus, born of Mary, finally subdues and conquers "that old serpent, the devil" before sending him to his everlasting punishment.

2) The Old Testament Law with its laborious system of blood sacrifices in the Old Testament expressed

the seriousness of sin and the penalty of eternal death it deserved. Its repetitive nature showed our powerlessness to decisively deal with the world's most incurable problem – the darkness in every human heart. But, more than that, the extortionate cost in the life of livestock also prefigures the perfect and permanent atonement that Jesus would make for the sins of the world when the blood of his innocent life was shed on the cross.

3) The Old Testament Prophets repeatedly called for a response of righteous living from the people of their generation - and they were rejected time and time again. This depressing reading consistently matches the observation in the New Testament that absolutely no one is justified (declared 'not guilty') because absolutely everyone falls short of God's standard.

4) The Old Testament Writings all yearn for someone who will satisfy the hungers of the human soul. Every bewildering circle in the Old Testament is magnificently squared in the New Testament in the person of Jesus.

This coherent, central narrative running through the Scriptures helps to resolve some of the biggest puzzles in the Bible.

For example, reading through Exodus, Leviticus and Numbers, many people in our day are shocked by the primitive nature of the legislation (in fact, it was revolutionary and strikingly humane compared with other legal codes from that time). But what use does a Christian have for it in the 21st Century Western world?

Consider the many offences which carried the death penalty in the Jewish Law of Moses. Isn't this all we need to know to dismiss the Bible as irrelevant to the issues of our age? The death penalty under the Law of Moses was prescribed for seventeen different offences.[54] Why do we not feel obliged to apply capital punishment to such, or indeed any, offenses in so-called Christian countries?

Because of Jesus who, in his own words, came not to abolish but *fulfil* the Law. What does that mean? Two things. First, that the death penalty is permanently valid because, however much our standards vary from age to age, all those sins listed above still constitute a serious offence against a holy God and always will. But second, because Jesus died for the sin of the whole world, *he has already paid the death penalty for all sin*. He has totally satisfied all the righteous requirements of the Law – including its draconian sanctions.

When Scripture interprets Scripture in this way all the pieces of the sometimes perplexing puzzle fall into place and the magnificent picture emerges. That's why it's important to be very cautious when attacking the Bible because of some appalling episode in its pages. Context is everything. Yes, there's war, abuse, adultery, rape, brutality, famine, pestilence, and much more besides in there but they are like the darker shapes in a giant collage that tells you the truth about human life and reveals God's magnificent plan to redeem it.

The unity and coherence of the Bible are amazing. As I argued in chapter 14, the resurrection stands out as stunning evidence of the truthfulness of Christianity. But, more than that, it fits perfectly and surprisingly into the logic of the big theme of the Bible. As J. John and Chris Walley write:

> "The resurrection of Jesus… is like one of those twists in a novel or film that takes you by surprise until you think about it, and then you realize that it actually makes sense and it fits with the plot. So the Old Testament teaches that death is the inevitable consequence of human beings having sinned against God. The interesting implication of this, which no one appears to have explored before the resurrection, is that if someone who had never sinned actually did die, death would have no hold over them."[55]

My conclusion to all this is that a book with so many diverse authors, writing over such a long period of time, could surely only display such unity and coherence if their work was commissioned and collated by one divine editor.

That's why I believe, along with the majority of Christians down the ages, that the Bible is God's inspired word; a trustworthy revelation about life, the universe and everything.

You might have thought that, with such a humanly inexplicable unity, the Bible would command the respect, if not the admiration, of those who are not believers. But no book has been as hated, as burned and as banned throughout history as this one has. That it has survived at all let alone remained against all odds easily the world's bestselling and most fervently sought-after book is what the next chapter is about.

Chapter 16

THE WORDS THAT WON'T GO AWAY

Many buildings, artefacts, writings and other items of historical interest have been lost without trace over the years. But **the Bible has suffered, withstood and overcome centuries of unparalleled attack. Its survival and success against the odds are quite remarkable.**

In July 1994 I travelled up a long and winding road in the wild and beautiful Cévennes in Southern France. There is a museum at the end of the road in the middle of nowhere called *le Musée du Désert*. It bears testimony to the large community of Huguenots who fled and hid in that rugged terrain following the revocation of the Edict of Nantes in 1685 by Louis XIV, ending a period of tolerance towards Protestants. One of the features of the museum is a display of tiny Bibles that were printed at that time, some small enough to be successfully concealed in a woman's hair. The Bible was absolutely forbidden in those days and, in peril of their lives, many people made inordinate efforts to safeguard it from obliteration.

It has occurred to me many times since that visit that the Bible must easily be the most consistently and passionately opposed book of all time. As A. W. Pink noted; "For two thousand years man's hatred of the Bible has been persistent, determined, relentless and murderous. Every possible effort has been made to undermine faith in the inspiration and authority of the Bible and innumerable enterprises have been undertaken with the determination to consign it to oblivion."[56]

No army has ever gone into action to either impose it on unwilling readers or defend it by force. Its principal endorsement and sole defence have been the love and esteem in which it is held by ordinary people who have read it and been transformed by its message. There are billions of us. It is easily the best-selling and most translated book in world history. At least one book of the Bible has been translated into over 2,500 languages. As an indication of the scale of that achievement, the publishing phenomenon that is J. K. Rowling's *Harry Potter* has at the time of writing been translated into less than seventy.

And yet, despite its popularity, the Bible is surely the most banned, burned, ridiculed and smeared book ever published. Why does the Bible polarise opinion like no other publication? I'll offer an answer at the end of this piece, but first of all I want to trace the extraordinary history of hatred towards the Christian Scriptures.

It started in the Roman Empire. On 24th February 303, the Emperor Diocletian published his *Edict Against the Christians,* ordering the burning of Bibles, the demolition of places of worship and issuing a blanket ban on Christians assembling to pray. This was the last great wave of Roman persecution against Christians but the first to explicitly target the Bible itself as well as those who read it.

Of course the Christian Scriptures in those days were all painstakingly copied by hand. There were no printing presses so the production of even one Bible would take many months. But despite Diocletian's bonfires, the Bible prevailed.

After the Roman Empire declined, the Bible was zealously censored by a lamentable political corruption of Christianity we call Christendom. The period we now call the European Dark Ages lasted for about a thousand years (5th-15th Centuries). During this time learning was stifled, the arts were suffocated, social progress ground to a snail's pace and, with Christianity sick and separated from its main source of inspiration, Islam was born.

(As an aside, I would argue that, had the Bible been available to ordinary Christians during the Dark Ages, none of the above would have happened; education would have been encouraged, the arts would have flourished, social progress would have accelerated and Islam would never have filled the vacuum left by a corrupt and ailing church, unrecognisable from that of the 1st Century. Incidentally, it's also worth pointing out that the crusades occurred at a time when the Bible was not publicly available. So people were denied the opportunity to read plainly that taking up the sword to spread faith, or even defend it, is contrary to the teaching of Jesus).

The American sociologist, author and pastor Tony Campolo was once reported to have mused about how Christendom had been a bad idea. "Mixing the church and state" he said, "is like mixing ice cream with cow manure. It may not do much to the manure, but it sure messes up the ice cream!" Quite so.

Various Councils from the time of Christendom stamped on calls for the Bible to be made available to the masses. They expressly forbade the translation of the Bible from Latin, thereby limiting its readership to the rich and powerful, who were eager to preserve their privileges at all costs. Canon 14 of the Council of Toulouse (1229), Canon 2 of the Council of Tarragona (1234) and Rules on Prohibited Books from the Council of Trent (1545-63) are three examples of this. In fact, *even priests* were usually denied access to the Scriptures for personal study.

But towards the end of the Dark Ages, people rose up to reclaim the Bible. Dissenters began to argue that it should be available to everyone, unshackled from Latin, and rendered in the language of the marketplace. At that time, restrictive suppression of the Scriptures gave way to violent attack on them.

John Wycliffe (c.1320–1384) was the first to attempt to translate the Bible into English, though it was from the Latin and not from the Hebrew and Greek source texts. The Council of Constance (1414-1418) later declared Wycliffe a heretic, banned his writings and trashed his work. As an insult to his legacy and as a warning to any admirers, his remains were exhumed and burned. Wycliffe's followers, called Lollards, were also burned at the stake with their Bibles hanging round their necks.

The scholarly William Tyndale (c.1494–1536) worked painstakingly, and at great personal cost, to produce the first English-language Bible translated directly from the original Hebrew and Greek. In his day it was a capital offence not only to translate the Scriptures into English but even to read or own such a translation or any part of it. He spent many months of his life in hiding, having to travel clandestinely around Belgium, the Netherlands and Germany to evade arrest and arrange for Bibles to be printed. They were smuggled into Britain hidden in bails of wool. In the end, Tyndale was betrayed, captured, tried and strangled to death before his remains were burned at the stake. His last words were "Lord, open the King of England's eyes!"

Many others were publicly executed at this time; most were burned alive. But the Bible was now available all over England and throughout Continental Europe on the black market. The lion was out of the cage.

Fierce opposition to the Bible spread like a rash all over Europe. But little by little, Bibles became available in more and more languages as the Reformation took hold. The long and severe intellectual, artistic, cultural and social winter of the Dark Ages started to thaw as the Bible began to influence culture once again.

But God's word then came under another form of attack; an assault on its authority through higher criticism. Enlightenment scholars in the universities and seminaries of the 18th and 19th Centuries began to erode confidence in the Bible's divine inspiration and authority. It was dismissed as inaccurate, unreliable and exaggerated. It was patronised as primitive legend, fable, and myth. It was disparaged as a human fabrication and rejected as revelation from God. Such attacks continue to the present day.

Of course, selective reading of the Bible was nothing new. Augustine of Hippo (354-430) once said "If you believe what you like in the Gospels, and reject what you don't like, it is not the gospel you believe, but yourself." But at this time in history higher criticism was a full-frontal attack on the authority of Scripture just as it was becoming freely available everywhere.

Christians who believe in the devil should be under no illusion why the Bible has been so ferociously opposed throughout history. It is in the interests of the enemies of Christ to keep the Holy Scriptures firmly shut. For wherever Christianity is vigorous, growing, mission-minded and healthy, the Bible tends to be held in high esteem and is centre stage. It is not for nothing that all the great revivals -from the Great Awakening in New England, to the Wesleyan movement that transformed 18th Century Britain, to the 1905 Welsh revival, to the Azusa Street Pentecostal outpouring in Los Angeles- *all* held tenaciously to the inspiration and authority of Scripture. Conversely, wherever the Bible is marginalised and scoffed at, the churches associated tend to slide into decline and irrelevance.

In more recent times, the Bible has been opposed and forbidden by atheist political dictatorships such as the former Soviet Union and present-day North Korea. It has been denounced and barred by Islamic theocracies such as Saudi Arabia, Yemen, the Maldives and Afghanistan. The Gideons list eighteen countries where they are not allowed to operate at all. There are many other countries where severe though not outright restrictions are imposed. Increasingly, their work is resisted in Western nations, for example recent reports in Canada and the UK, to avoid "causing offence" to people of other faiths.

Has any other book in human history sparked as much opposition and antagonism? It's hard to think of anything that comes close. And yet the Bible not only survives, it prevails. Even in secular countries where the Bible's obituary was written long ago, it refuses to go away. As recently as June 2013, for example, it stormed back up the best-seller lists in Norway, knocking *Fifty Shades of Grey* off the top spot.[57]

The Bible itself asserts its invincibility. 2,750 years ago the Prophet Isaiah declared:

> *The grass withers and the flowers fall, but the word of our God endures forever."*
>
> Isaiah 40.8.

And Jesus said:

> *Heaven and earth will pass away, but my words will never pass away."*
>
> Matthew 24.35.

Like Daniel and his contemporaries emerging unscathed from Nebuchadnezzar's furnace without a hair singed or even the smell of fire on them (see Daniel 3), the Bible continues to stand unflinching, untainted and undiminished by every angry attack on it. Its stubborn survival and ever-enduring popularity are a near miracle.

So why does the Bible divide opinion like no other book?

Perhaps it is uniquely hated and attacked because it tells the full, unpalatable truth about human nature. We are sinners in need of a Saviour. And human pride and ego rage against the very idea that we need to be saved from ourselves and from the folly of our rebellion against God.

Furthermore, no other book spells out so clearly the devil's ultimate fate; he will be judged and thrown into a lake of fire prepared for him (Revelation 20.10) and he unleashes his fury against the book that affirms it. No wonder that virtually throughout the history of Christianity the Bible has been burned, suppressed, outlawed, belittled and undermined.

And, conversely, I think the Bible is loved and treasured like no other book because its central message of God's love and grace is *such good news*. It transforms millions of lives like no other book ever can, ever has done and ever will. That's what the next chapter is all about.

PART 2

Because it works

Chapter 17

IT DOES WHAT IT SAYS ON THE TIN

Having noted the extraordinary unity of the Bible's message and its impressive resilience, the other thing that stands out for me about this book is its power to change the lives for the better of people who read it with an open mind. Put simply, **the message of the Bible delivers.**

I once knew an old American man called Frank Whitmarsh who married and settled in France after serving in the U. S. Army in the Normandy landings. If you've seen the film *Saving Private Ryan*, you'll have a graphic idea of the carnage he survived as he made his way up Omaha Beach on 6th June 1944. Each soldier in that operation had been issued a pocket New Testament. Frank tucked his into the breast pocket of his uniform and forgot about it.

As a young man, by his own admission, Frank was a fairly cynical, hard swearing, heavy drinking kind of guy with no time for spiritual things. But shortly after that harrowing battle to breach the Nazi defences just north of Colleville-sur-Mer everything changed.

Frank still had that same New Testament some sixty years after D-Day; it was just about intact but was badly damaged. It had in fact been the shield that stood between an enemy bullet hitting him straight through the heart. Between assault battles Frank began to read the damaged pages of his little pocket New Testament and it started a surprising journey of faith for him.

Why does the Bible change lives? Over the years, people who have read it with an open mind have found that it confronts, provokes and convicts them. It soothes, assures and consoles troubled hearts. It brings guidance, wisdom, light and peace of mind to enquiring minds. It fires up the spiritual side of people in gratitude and joy, nourishing faith and brings health to the soul.

I've found that so many of those who read it often and take heed of what it says are people who "have it together." As Charles H. Spurgeon once put it "A Bible that's falling apart usually belongs to someone who isn't."

There are many people I could write about whose lives have been turned round *just by reading the Bible and believing its message* but I am going to have to be savagely selective.

I love the story of Elliott Osowitt.[58] Born into a liberal Jewish family, Elliott worked in the tourism industry and his frequent travels away from home led him to years of what he calls "loose living and immorality." Things unravelled in his domestic life until he lost control. One of his two daughters started to get into trouble and ended up in prison during that time. On Christmas Eve 1996 his wife Polly, fed up with the impact her husband's lifestyle was having on their children, threw him out of the house.

Elliott, depressed and disconsolate as he reflected on the mess his life had become, was going to turn a gun on himself in his motel room that night. Before he did though, he noticed an open Gideons Bible laying on the television set.

"When I looked at it," he says, "I thought who needs that? and I threw it on the floor. It fell on the floor and it still stayed open, like it was beckoning me. It really made me mad, so I kicked it, but it hit this wooden box frame under the bed and popped back on the floor."

So he picked the book up and was about to hurl it at the wall when he glanced down and saw a verse from the Gospel of John.

> *Peace I leave with you; my peace I give you. I do not give to you as the world gives. Do not let your hearts be troubled and do not be afraid.*
>
> John 14.27.

Inexplicably, Elliott stopped and welled up. That night began a long process of change and healing that eventually led to reconciliation with his entire family and his life getting back on track. "Although God is still doing a work in my family and me, we are now a recovering, reconciled, restored, and most of all, a resurrected family" he says. Elliott Osowitt now leads a church called Faith Fellowship in Jefferson, North Carolina. That's the sort of thing I mean when I say that the message of the Bible touches and changes lives.

Then consider Richard Taylor. There are clear parallels between his and Elliott's stories though they come from very different backgrounds. As a teenager growing up without a father figure in his life, Richard lived an existence of crime and drug addiction in South Wales for which he served several sentences in H. M. Prison Swansea. One night, in jail awaiting conviction and sentencing, he picked up the Gideons Bible that had been placed in his cell and tore out a page to roll a cigarette. This is how he explains what happened next:

> "I opened the Bible randomly and tore out a page and made myself a roll-up. I struck the match, but suddenly, I found that I had an inner voice that I wasn't used to hearing. It said *This is all wrong, I should be reading this, not putting a match to it.* I blew the match out, unrolled the page, and began to read it. It was the Gospel of

John chapter 1. I read the page and then read most of that Gospel, about twenty chapters, before I put it down. I found it captivating. I was lying on my bunk with the Bible resting on my chest and fell asleep. Sleeping in prison is not easy because of the noise and I wasn't on any drugs – my usual way of drifting off to sleep. Nevertheless, I slept the deepest and most peaceful sleep that I could remember. From early afternoon, right through to the next morning, I slept. It was as if the weariness of years of turmoil, crime, drugs, aggression and fighting was being rolled away through peaceful sleep. My subconscious mind was being cleared of the nightmares of my life up to now. The Bible talks about the peace of God that passes anyone's understanding and perhaps this was my first experience of it."[59]

Richard was then inexplicably spared a heavy sentence on condition that he spent some time in a Christian rehabilitation centre which he agreed to. By then his life had already been turned around and he is now one of the country's most dynamic and influential church leaders.

The Police Chief who had no control over Taylor in his days of spiralling crime can only admit that he is a reformed man and happily wrote an endorsement on the cover of Taylor's autobiography *To Catch a Thief*. Taylor's church has many reformed criminals, drug addicts, ex-lap dancers, alcoholics and the like so it's a very colourful place!

Two examples of lives turned around by the message of the Bible. And yet some want to outlaw the distribution of Gideons Bibles in schools, hotels and prisons for fear either of offending people from other faiths or upsetting touchy atheists.

The Bible is immensely valued by those for whom the government suppresses its distribution.

Former barrister and now leader of the Church of England's largest church, Nicky Gumbel, once travelled to Communist Russia when he was 21, at a time when the Bible was forbidden there. He visited a church in Samarkand, central Asia, wondering who he might give his Russian Bibles to. It was a risk because such churches were often infiltrated by KGB agents. He saw a man who was about 65 years old and who had a radiant expression on his face. Gumbel thought he looked full of the Holy Spirit so he followed him out of the church, touched him on the shoulder and handed one of his Bibles to him.

When the old man saw a whole Russian Bible, he was elated. He took out of his pocket a thread-bare New Testament. It had been read over and over until it was completely worn out. Now he had a whole Bible in his own language. He didn't speak any English and Gumbel didn't speak a word of Russian but they hugged each other with overflowing joy. This book would help sustain the old man's faith in the most hostile circumstances.

The organisation Open Doors has thousands of similar stories after years of smuggling Bibles into closed Marxist and Islamic states. The Bible seems to sustain that striking faith which violent and oppressive regimes can't extinguish.

But the Bible's impact on people's lives isn't limited to just personal salvation or private encouragement. It also makes a difference to the way ordinary people lead their lives and, directly and indirectly, has a huge effect on society.

It's when the Church shakes off its pompous traditions and gets back to the simplicity of the Bible's message that it becomes truly transformative. The Archbishop of Canterbury Justin Welby made headline news in July 2013 for saying that local churches, facilitating not-for-profit Credit Unions, will aim to put payday loan companies that take advantage of the poor out of business. Where does that come from? It comes from Old Testament prophets like Isaiah:

> *The Lord takes his place in court;*
> *he rises to judge the people.*
> *The Lord enters into judgment*
> *against the elders and leaders of his people:*
> *'It is you who have ruined my vineyard;*

> *the plunder from the poor is in your houses.*
> *What do you mean by crushing my people*
> *and grinding the faces of the poor?'*
> *declares the Lord, the Lord Almighty.*
>
> Isaiah 3.13-15.

And it comes from the New Testament as well with Jesus saying things like:

> *When you give a luncheon or dinner, do not invite your friends, your brothers or relatives, or your rich neighbours; if you do, they may invite you back and so you will be repaid. But when you give a banquet, invite the poor, the crippled, the lame, the blind, and you will be blessed. Although they cannot repay you, you will be repaid at the resurrection of the righteous.*
>
> Luke 14.12-14.

An article in *The Daily Telegraph* in February 2013 found that 6,500 Church of England parishes now provide special services for elderly people, schoolchildren, parents and new immigrants.[60] 8 out of 10 individual parishioners give up their spare time to provide informal help to people struggling with issues such as isolation, family breakdown, drug abuse, domestic violence or spiralling debt. And that's just the Church of England, not including other churches.

According to the 2012 National Church and Social Action Survey[61] Christians offer *98 million hours* of unpaid volunteer work on social projects every year - and that's *outside* of church based activities like lunch clubs and youth groups. There seems to be something about the message of grace that motivates Bible-reading Christians to serve others and make the world a better place.

The online satirical news source *The Onion* did a piece on this in January 2014 in a report on a local church outreach in Macon, Georgia;

"Sources confirmed today that the brainwashed morons at First Baptist Assembly of Christ, all of whom blindly accept whatever simplistic fairy tales are fed to them, volunteer each Wednesday night to provide meals to impoverished members of the community. 'Unfortunately, there are a lot of people in town who have fallen on hard times and are unable to afford to put food on the table, so we try to help out as best we can,' said 48-year-old Kerri Bellamy, one of the mindless sheep who adheres to a backward ideology and is incapable of thinking for herself, while spooning out homemade shepherd's pie to a line of poor and homeless individuals. As of press time, the brainless, unthinking lemmings had donated winter clothing to several needy families and still hadn't opened their eyes to reality."[62]

I once conducted a survey amongst the non-churchgoing parents who brought their children to a holiday club that one of the churches I lead put on. One of the questions was "Should All Saints' be doing more in the community?" 80% answered along the lines of, "it already does an awful lot."16% confessed they didn't know. 4% felt the church should do more. Of these, one person thought we use the building too much for church programmes and not enough for non-church activities. I wondered if that was like saying "Why isn't Old Trafford used more for rock concerts, instead of stupid football matches?" Someone else confessed to be an atheist and said we should be tidying elderly people's gardens. On reflection, I wish I had had the presence of mind to reply "Oh, there's no need for that; there are volunteers from the British Atheist Association already doing that all over the country when they're not running events like this!"

I am not saying here that people who don't look to the Bible as their inspiration make no difference in society. That is obviously untrue. I am just saying that, *overwhelmingly*, the message of the Bible touches lives and changes society for the better.

Sociologist Robert Woodberry spent over ten years researching the effect of "conversionary Protestant" missionaries on the countries where they served before reaching this stunning conclusion: "Areas where Protestant missionaries had a significant presence in the past are on average more economically developed today, with comparatively better health, lower infant mortality, lower corruption, greater literacy, higher educational attainment (especially for women), and more robust membership in non-governmental associations."[63]

I want the world to be a better place and the book that Christians believe to be inspired has a proven track record of transforming those who read it with an open mind.

If you're one of those people you'll know exactly what I mean. If you're not, I hope you at least you will acknowledge that the message of the Bible has proved to be overwhelmingly good for society. And the next time you open the Bible, why not ask God to speak to you through it? – it might lead to an adventure you'd never imagine possible.

Chapter 18

LOOKING THE LAST ENEMY IN THE EYE

These last nine chapters are more personal and are based more on my experiences. As I've said before, my conversion was experiential - emotional even - and I only came to think through the logic of my faith afterwards. I would have said when I was 17 that I am a Christian because I have experienced something like nothing else I have ever known. That hasn't changed. But I say now that I am a Christian *first of all* because I think Christianity is true, and I think that there is good evidence to support it that you can examine yourself. Only secondly do I say that I'm a Christian because it works for me.

But work for me it certainly does. My experience of Christ is real. He is not like an imaginary friend (though I struggled to make friends as a child I never invented one) nor is God like Father Christmas or the tooth fairy or anything of the sort. I worked out that these were fictitious at the age of about 6 and Kathie and I resolved never to mislead our children by encouraging them to ever think they were real.

The first thing from my personal experience that inclines me to being a Christian comes from accompanying Christians in their final days and being involved in their funerals. **Watching Christians die confident and unafraid is inspirational and has left a profound mark on me.**

The Baptist preacher David Pawson sometimes speaks about a man he knew in Beaconsfield, Buckinghamshire who was told that he had only a few weeks to live. He took the news calmly, thanked the doctor and returned home. He then sent out invitations to all his non-Christian friends. The invitations read "Come and stay with me. Come and see how a Christian dies!"

I have had the privilege of visiting Christians who know that their battle with serious illness is going to result in imminent death. Generally, they don't feel that "beating cancer" means staying alive. As John Piper puts it in his little booklet *Don't Waste Your Cancer*[64] "Satan designs to destroy our love for Christ. God designs to deepen our love for Christ. Cancer does not win if we die. It wins if we fail to cherish Christ."

I remember vividly one woman smiling gently and saying to me: "I don't much care for leaving my friends *just* now but I'm not afraid at all. I know I'm going to a wonderful place." I would travel to see her wondering what I might say that might be of any comfort. I would come home feeling that the visit had been more beneficial to me than to her.

Her funeral was a tremendous celebration of her life but it contained an appropriate expression of our grief at parting. The abiding memory for me was a rousing "There is a Redeemer" – a song she had specifically requested.

> *When I stand in glory*
> *I shall see His face*
> *And there I'll serve my King forever*
> *In that holy place.*

Christian funerals have a quality about them that is unique. What I mean here is funerals arranged for committed Christians rather than funerals with Christian elements for people who have only vague notions of the gospel and probably haven't been near a church except as guests at weddings or baptisms. In genuine Christian funerals - yes, there are tears but they are usually a release of emotion and gratitude, not bitterness and certainly not anger. Overwhelmingly there is a sense of victory, of triumph, and of homecoming.

And in Christian writing, death is often referred to as sleep – something to wake up from refreshed in the light of a brand new day.

> *Brothers and sisters, we do not want you to be uninformed about those who sleep in death, so that you do not grieve like the rest of mankind, who have no hope. For we believe that Jesus died and rose again, and so we believe that God will bring with Jesus those who have fallen asleep in him.*
>
> 1 Thessalonians 4.13-14.

Another beautiful death happened about a year earlier from the one I mentioned on the previous page; another woman with a strong and radiant faith. On her death bed, she gathered friends round and lifted her voice in praise with them in the week she died. I'm told they exhausted the entire hymn book and felt uplifted, grateful and full of joy as they sung happily of Christ's incomparable glories and grace.

Strangely enough, about halfway between those two deaths, I was asked to visit a man who was not a Christian but who wished to see a priest before dying. He was quite frail when I saw him. He had been a critic of Christianity and had evidently made decisions in his life that he now regretted. I noticed *The God Delusion* in his bookshelf; though it was full of books, the spine of that book caught my eye among the other volumes.

He was resigned to the inevitability of death, somewhat forlorn and manifestly not at peace. That's why he had asked to see me. We talked for about an hour, mostly about matters personal to him, and he accepted my offer to pray with him at the end. Though he was evidently wealthy, it was quite pathetic that he had only recently seemed to realise that he wasn't able to take anything with him. As they say, there's no prize for being the richest man in the cemetery. It was remarkable how a spiritual sense of stillness and calm settled in the room as we prayed. I think he felt it too but I do not know whether he made his peace with God before he died. I hope so.

In the Anglican Service of Ordination, the Bishop reads a list of things that newly ordained ministers are expected to do and it includes "they are to minister to the sick and prepare the dying for their death." I have found it a great honour to accompany people at the end of life and I am rarely unmoved by the experience. It is, in short, an inspiration to my faith in Christ and it affirms his authority over death in my experience.

I am in good company. The British historian and author A. N. Wilson became a cause celebre amongst sceptics when his withering attacks on Christianity followed his public embracing of atheism. But around April 2009, Wilson stunned his readers by returning to Christianity, celebrating Easter at his local church. He wrote about his U-turn in a national newspaper and I understand exactly where he is coming from:

> "My own return to faith has surprised none more than myself… my belief has come about in

large measure because of the lives and examples of people I have known, not the famous, not saints but friends and relations who have lived and faced death in light of the resurrection story, or in the quiet acceptance that they have a future after they die."[65]

Simon Guillebaud's book *Dangerously Alive* is a collection of diary entries and newsletters from his time as a frontier missionary in genocidal Burundi. At the time he lived there (1998-2009) it was the most dangerous place to live on earth. The scale of human depravity recorded in that book makes for sobering reading. But Guillebaud, along with other Christian ministries like Scripture Union, Tearfund, Youth for Christ and Partners Trust International, made a huge humanitarian and spiritual impact on that country, most of the time in peril of his own life. Here's one passage that is typical:

"I sped around the bend in the road on my motorbike, but quickly scrambled to a stop, surprised to see a figure in the middle of the road, just ahead of me. He was holding a grenade in his hand, ready to blow me up. I knew this for a fact - he had made his intentions clear two days before when he'd written saying he was going to cut out my eyes. I'd had sleepless nights over the threat, of course, but I'd gone to stay at someone else's place for a while and was varying my routes around town so that he wouldn't know where to lie in wait for me. My guard waved at me - a pre-arranged sign not to approach. This was both surreal and yet chillingly real. God, what on earth shall I do? If it has to be, I'm ready to die. Let's go..."[66]

In February 2015, twenty-one Christian men in their prime, members of the Coptic Church in Egypt, were dressed in orange jumpsuits, their hands were tied behind their backs, they were lined up on a beach, forced to their knees and were all simultaneously beheaded by masked men in black standing behind them. These men were humble, Egyptian labourers who had travelled across the border to Libya to earn a living and provide for their families.

I did not have the stomach to watch the footage which was widely circulated on the Internet, but I did see some stills of the men shortly before they were killed. They must have known exactly what was coming but their bodies were not tensed up in fear. Their faces did not appear to be cringing, fearful or even nervous. They all looked strangely at peace. At prayer probably... Those who have watched the video of the execution have commented that you could hear some of the men call out the words "O Lord Jesus!" as the beheading started.

For me, to live is Christ; to die is gain.
                                                    Philippians 1.21.

Put alongside what atheist Bertrand Russell said before his death, it is no surprise which philosophy draws me and which one leaves me cold. Russell said: "There is darkness without and when I die there will be darkness within. There is no splendour, no vastness anywhere, only triviality for a moment, and then nothing."[67]

But Christians do not hope against hope when it comes to death. The Bible teaches that people are saved from hell and eternal death not on the basis of the good things they have done but on the basis of the perfect life Christ has lived.

As John Wesley said of his conversion experience: "I felt my heart strangely warmed. I felt I did trust in Christ, Christ alone for salvation; and *an assurance was given me* that he had taken away my sins, even mine, and saved me from the law of sin and death."[68] (My italics).

That's why Christians have assurance of salvation and perfect peace in death.

That's why a young, pretty mother-of-two Rachel Barkey was able to speak so confidently just four months before her untimely death from cancer at the age of 37 in 2009. Her moving speech is on YouTube and a simple search of her name will give you a link to the video. As you can see if you watch the video, she is not in denial; she is clearly emotional about having to leave her husband and young children so soon. But the overwhelming theme of her address is gratitude.

This is the way I want to die when my time comes. And that's the 18th reason I am a Christian.

How do you want to die? In denial by constantly putting the question to the back of your mind even as the end draws near? Where's the wisdom in putting off thinking about all this until old age sets in?

None of us knows for sure when our life will end. If yesterday was an average day, 150,000 people died. I'm guessing most of them had plans for the following week.

Chapter 19

WHEN THE SLEEPING GIANT STIRS

One of the things I love hearing about most is revival. It's the nineteenth reason I'm a Christian. **Revivals around the world attest to the continuing and awesome power of the gospel.**

In April 2013, reports started circulating about some unusual and exciting goings-on in a Pentecostal fellowship called Victory Church in Cwmbran, South Wales. In one of their midweek prayer meetings (10th April) a man called Paul, who had been wheelchair-bound and in constant pain for ten years following a road traffic accident, was suddenly and dramatically healed, following prayer for his condition. The 70 or so people who were there looked on startled before bursting into spontaneous applause and cheering as Paul picked up his wheelchair, held it high above his head and began to walk around the church.

On 15th May I made the four-hour journey down to Cwmbran with a couple of friends to experience for myself the ongoing excitement in that place. For over a month they had been seeing dozens of people converted to Christ every night, often with claims of an accompanying and immediate release from depression, self-harm, addictions and so on.

When I got there half an hour before the meeting started, I was surprised to see that a long queue had formed. I had never before seen a crowd of people queuing for up to an hour to get into church. There were enthusiastic cheers and a gentle, orderly surge to get in to the auditorium as soon as the doors opened. It felt a bit like the January sales.

Inside, there was nothing particularly lovely about the building - rather the opposite; it is a functional, modern, converted retail outlet. There was nothing especially amazing about the band and nothing out of the ordinary about the presentation and preaching. They were good, and I appreciated them, but it was honestly nothing exceptional. So I was impressed when a short, simple, unadorned, almost restrained presentation of the gospel was met immediately by about twenty people leaving their seats to go forward and commit their lives to following Christ.

I have to say that the atmosphere was passionate and intense but there was no crowd manipulation, no theatrics, no pressure and certainly no big appeal for money. I want to insist that what I experienced was nothing to do with hype or a worked-up atmosphere.

The basic difference between what I experienced there and what I usually see in church was an increased awareness of *God's presence*. It's very difficult to explain or describe. The presence of God is something you encounter on a deeper level than thoughts and feelings.

Later in the meeting, another decent but unremarkable talk, without notes from (of all places) Leviticus 14 brought a conviction of sin upon virtually everyone there, including me. At the invitation, hundreds came forward seeking cleansing from God through the blood of Christ. I suppose it was the *vividness* of knowing I needed forgiveness from God and should eagerly ask for it that was most unusual. It was one of those few times in life when, in trying to put something into words for someone, I'd say "To be honest, you'd really have to *be there* to understand what I'm talking about."

Every six weeks or so at Victory Church they were baptizing a group of 50-100 new believers. There were further reports of remarkable, unexplained healings as the thing they called "The Welsh Outpouring" continued to roll on. Their excellent church website claimed "Hundreds have come in as atheists, backslidden, lost, addicted, rich, poor, confused, self-harming etc and gone out loving Jesus as He has reached them."

What they experienced in Cwmbran was not a movement on the scale of a great revival or awakening, and they acknowledged this openly. And like all such movements, the intensity has no doubt faded over time, but being there gave me an idea of what a full-scale revival -an amplified version of the outpouring in Cwmbran- must be like.

The Baptist theologian John Piper in his book *A Godward Life* wrote about revival, defining it as "The sovereign work of God to awaken his people with fresh intensity to the truth and glory of God, the ugliness of sin, the horror of hell, the preciousness of Christ's atoning work, the wonder of salvation by grace through faith, the urgency of holiness and witness, and the sweetness of worship with God's people."[69]

That's quite an occurrence! And every now and again, quite unpredictably, though usually after a season of sustained intercessory prayer, revival breaks out somewhere on earth. Here are some examples:

- In the 16th Century, the Reformation spread like a wildfire throughout Europe as thousands became alive to God through discovering the magnificent doctrine of justification by faith.

- The brutally persecuted *Camisards* in 17th Century France grew exponentially; from nowhere, they rapidly accounted for 10% of the population of

France. They rediscovered spiritual gifts such as speaking in tongues and healing; some of their infants would prophesy the wonders of God though they were barely old enough to string sentences together.

- The Great Awakening associated with Jonathan Edwards in New England (1730s and 1740s) was an important movement in which people *en masse* cried out to God, begging for mercy such was their heightened awareness of the immediate danger of hell and the urgent necessity of being saved through faith in Jesus.

- The Methodist Revival, marked by John Wesley's inspirational preaching and Charles Wesley's rousing hymns, changed the face of 18th Century Britain. It has often been said that this revival, accompanied by the sweeping social reforms of Christian visionaries like Lord Shaftesbury and William Wilberforce, kept Britain from the kind of political turmoil that resulted in the blood-soaked, anti-theist French Revolution across the channel.

- The 1905 Welsh Revival, (some date it to 1904) associated with former collier Evan Roberts, was a sweeping movement in which the pubs emptied and the chapels swelled in a matter of months. 100,000 people were converted in less than a year.

Crime came to a virtual standstill. Councils held emergency meetings to discuss what to do with the police who suddenly had nothing to do all day. The number of children born to unmarried parents dropped 44% within a year of the beginning of the revival. It is said that the ponies that worked down the mines were confused and didn't know what to do as they were used to responding to daily physical brutality and hearing orders in foul language. Both fell into rapid disuse as coal miners were converted in droves.

- The Azusa Street Outpouring beginning in April 1906 grew rapidly into the fastest growing religious movement on earth; Pentecostalism. Thousands of church leaders from all over the world visited Azusa Street, Los Angeles between 1906 and 1908 and exported this fiery, passionate expression of Christianity everywhere they went. There are over 500 million Pentecostals and Charismatics today and the movement is still growing fast.

- The East African Revival of the 1920s and 30's dramatically altered the spiritual landscape of Uganda, Rwanda, Burundi, Kenya, Tanzania and Congo.

The Argentinian revival in the 1970s transformed sections of society, starting with the prisons.

There are dozens more well-documented examples.

- A friend of mine from the Church Mission Society recently visited Nepal and reported that the church is doubling in size in that country every two and a half years. It has gone from practically nobody to over one million people in just sixty years.

- Then what about South Korea? After years of bloody persecution, the church grew sharply post Second World War as a BBC news report showed in 2009.[70] According to the Korean Overseas Information Service, before 1945 approximately 2% of the Korean population was Christian. By 1991, less than half a century later, the figure had ballooned to 45%.

- China too has experienced extraordinary revival, with reports of amazing healings, even resurrections, since the outlawing of Christianity by the Communists. Brother Yun's book *The Heavenly Man* documents the cruel suffering of some Chinese Christians and the spectacular growth of the underground church there. According to Brook Lee writing in the *World Policy Journal* in 2012, the Chinese government acknowledges the existence of 14 million Christians in China, but it is widely believed that there are at least 70 million more than that. In fact, it is commonly claimed that there are more disciples of Jesus Christ in Communist China today than there are members of the Communist Party.

What all this says to me is that the gospel is still just as potent as it ever was when, in the first three centuries A.D., it took on the mighty Roman Empire, got absolutely battered with wave after wave of oppression and persecution - and then came out on top.

The gospel has extraordinary power to turn society's greatest ills on their head *by changing lives*. And sometimes, this occurs in a sweeping movement that not even the hardest opponent, the most defiant society or the most resistant government can suppress. The gospel is unstoppable, especially so in times of revival.

There is no way in my mind that, during these revivals, the numerous conversions are just the result of heightened emotions and mass manipulation, and that the healings associated are just psychosomatic, and that the resulting impact on society is just lots of people trying hard to be nice at the same time.

No, it seems to me that revivals are a sovereign work of God that demonstrate his supremacy and amazing grace, affording the world a temporary glimpse of both. In a sense, revivals are a foretaste of heaven.

This is the nineteenth reason I am a Christian. And I think it's telling that you never really hear sceptics bothering to research this amazing phenomenon, still less venturing to offer an explanation for it. I seem to read scoffing remarks every week on Internet forums about there being "no evidence" for Christian belief. Well, how about revivals for exhibit (a)?

All my Christian life I have prayed for renewal and revival; renewal for the church and revival for the world. I have probably heard hundreds of prayers for this in every church I have belonged to. It remains a deep yearning in my soul.

> *Lord, I have heard of your fame;*
> *I stand in awe of your deeds, Lord.*
> *Repeat them in our day,*
> *in our time make them known;*
> *in wrath remember mercy.*
>
> (Habakkuk 3.2)

Oh, that the church would wake up. And oh, that the world would taste and see how *good* the Lord is.

Chapter 20

NO PLACE LIKE HOME

Every summer Kathie and I head off on holiday somewhere and we never fail to check out the nearest lively church to visit while we are away.

I suppose, being a church leader, I rarely get the opportunity to sit in the congregation and enjoy the service without feeling responsible if the preacher is a bit long (I always keep to time, believe me), or if the guitar is slightly out of tune (that could be mine to be fair) or if the projection of words onto the screen is distractingly slow, or if the heating is not working. Or whatever... It's a pleasant change when all that is someone else's problem.

But what I love most about visiting other churches is that, wherever it might be on God's earth, and even though I probably don't know a soul, I always feel like I am with my *real family*. The nineteenth reason I am a Christian is that **Christian fellowship offers a depth and quality of relationship I have not found or enjoyed elsewhere.**

It doesn't even matter if I can't fully understand the language. I have worshipped with Japanese, Moroccan, Tamil, French and Filipino congregations and in each case I've barely understood a word. I picked up French in the end but when we first moved to France, I was lost.

No matter what the language might be, it hardly matters that the words are foreign to me. There is a language of heaven where mere vocabulary is secondary. There is a human connectedness in worship that goes deeper than the mind and the heart; it touches the soul of anyone who is alive to God through Jesus.

We used to sing a simple and delightful song when I was a church leader in France by Mady Ramos. I would love singing it because it articulates so guilelessly and so accurately what worshiping with other Christians feels like for me.

Moi, je suis dans la joie	I am filled of joy
quand on me dit :	when they say to me:
'Allons, allons à la maison	'Come on, let's go to the house
de l'Éternel.'	of the Lord.'
Là, sont réunis	There are gathered
mes frères et mes amis,	brothers, sisters, friends,
Tous, tous, tous	All
les gens que j'aime,	the people I love,
ceux qui me comprennent.	those who understand me.
C'est ici que je suis bien.	Here is where I feel good.

I would sometimes look round at other members of the church as we sang it and the smiles on people's faces assured me that I wasn't alone in feeling that *this is family*. It's where we can let the masks down, be ourselves and make mistakes in an atmosphere of love and acceptance.

But I wonder... Isn't this just a social phenomenon that works the same way in secular contexts? I know that people feel happiness and belonging when they meet up with friends in pubs and clubs. *I do*. I love the feeling of seeing people with whom I have a common interest.

Whenever I go to football matches it feels amazing to be part of a crowd cheering on my team and winding up the opposing fans. I love celebrating a goal or a penalty save – the feeling of elation, of solidarity, is thrilling. I love the banter with the opposing supporters as well. Singing "Is there a fire drill?" when my team goes 4-0 up and the other team's fans make for the exits in disgust is hilarious. But nothing compares with the strength of solidarity, the depth of friendship, the familial affection I have when I am with fellow believers. Everything else seems like a pale imitation.

I love it when someone becomes a Christian, or is baptized as an adult. In fact, few things bring me greater happiness. It is very similar of the birth of a baby. In a sense, *that's what it is*. This is why Jesus described beginning a new life of Christian faith as being "born again."

When people come to faith in Christ, they are born into a family of brothers and sisters. Any church anywhere in the world is a gathering of spiritual siblings. You can travel to any part of the world and there you will find believers in Jesus Christ who know what you mean when you celebrate his greatness or lament over the things that grieve him. There is an amazing connection between Christians even before meeting up.

Of course, brothers and sisters sometimes fall out. Church members fall out as well sometimes. But in both cases they remain brothers and sisters. That's one of the reasons Christians celebrate Holy Communion. When I partake of the Lord's Supper, it is a reminder of the essential unity before God with my brothers and sisters. This is where we bury our pride, forgive one another, renew our love for each other and for Christ. There is a bond, a connection, a unity which transcends language, culture, tradition and experience.

> *We, who are many, are one body, for we all partake of the one loaf.*
> 1 Corinthians 10.17.

I used to think that Christians were weird. When I was at Sixth Form College, I thought they always seemed a bit intense. I couldn't understand why they would enjoy meeting together as a Christian Union and do boring things like study the Bible and sing songs seated in a circle. I felt a bit sorry for them, like they were a self-help group for misfits and losers.

But after I became a Christian, I went to one of their meetings. I discovered that they were all quite normal. In fact, I found mostly that they were modest and beautiful people with amazing stories to tell. I found that I could completely relate to them. I began to look forward to Christian Union meetings more than anything else in the week.

The New Testament has a word for the kind of close friendship that Christians live out and enjoy. It's usually translated "fellowship" or "life together." In fact, the word is translated from the Greek *koinonia* which has many meanings and no single English word adequately express its range or depth. It comes from a word meaning "mutual" but it carries the sense of relationship, of joint participation in something with someone, of community, of sharing and even intimacy.

In Acts 2.44 and 45 it says: "All the believers were together and had everything in common. They sold property and possessions to give to anyone who had need."

John Stott in his commentary on Acts describes these verses as "disturbing." In a way they are, but I think there's something about the renunciation of possessiveness that is liberating and exhilarating.

When I was at Bible College in 1988 we gave away our much loved Citroen 2CV to a fellow student of very modest means. His need was greater than ours and God had already provided us with the funds for the larger model we needed for our expanding family. In 2008, about 6 months before we left Paris, a member in my church came up to me and said, "We're getting a new car. Would you like our old Mercedes!? You can sell it when you leave for England. We love you and we want to bless you." So you plant a *Deux Chevaux* and 20 years later you reap a Merc! It was not a brand new model but we felt like royalty driving around in it!

I mention this just to make the point that they are not isolated incidents. Because of the love there is between believers in Christ I have discovered that it is not all that rare for Christians to voluntarily give away books, washing machines, furniture, cars, even property when they could have sold them and kept the money. I find that many Christians are incredibly generous.

This may surprise you but in 2012, the most recent figures I have access to, Church of England parishes alone (not including other churches in England, let alone the rest of the United Kingdom, donated more money to other charitable organisations (£46m), than was raised through the BBC Children in Need telethon (£43.3m).[71] It doesn't surprise me. Discreet, unpretentious but excessive generosity is one of the marks of Christianity's authenticity and goodness. It is rarely mentioned in the media but perhaps that just highlights how genuine it is.

I've known Christians struggling to pay their bills checking the mail and finding anonymously posted envelopes full of banknotes. And, given the nature of the thing, I'm sure there's a lot that goes on that no one ever hears about. I love being a member of the God's people. No wonder pagan observers of the first Christians are recorded to have said, "Look, how they love one another and how they are ready to die for each other."

Especially in the West, people can sometimes fall into the trap of imagining that being a Christian is just "me and Jesus." But there are 44 different "one another's" in the New Testament. The church is a group of people who are commanded to love one other, forgive one another, mutually encourage one another, spur one another on, carry each other's burdens, accept one another, hold one another accountable, admonish one another, build one another up, bear with each other and so on.

There is virtually nothing in the New Testament about self-fulfilment. Christians are not voluntary members of a special interest club, still less a motley collection of individuals with private beliefs. Christians are citizens of a new community.

The Christian community is one in which my fellow believers and I can talk about things that really matter in our lives. When Christian community works like it is designed to -*koinonia*- people can ask me and I them "How are you *really*?" It is a depth of authentic friendship I have not experienced anywhere else – even amongst my own family members who are not Christians.

That's the 20th reason I am a Christian. It's special belonging to the biggest, happiest, craziest, most diverse family in the world. It's my *true* family and the key to my real identity; a child of God with brothers and sisters as numerous as the grains of sand on the shore and the stars in the sky.

Chapter 21

LIKE HEAVEN ON EARTH

In every life there are highs of exhilaration and lows of despair. We can't stay on a permanent high any more than we can live on top of Mount Everest. But one of the reasons I am a Christian is that so many of those peaks that punctuate most lives have been, in my case, sublime experiences of worship. **Foretastes of Heaven in worship are unlike any other earthly experience.**

Three years ago, one of the churches I lead had a special celebration to mark the end of a quite substantial building project, so we invited the architect, the boss of the building company and his workmen to join us so we could thank them for their work and offer them gifts to show our appreciation.

One of the contractors was clearly unfamiliar with church and was astounded by what he experienced; a puppet-led presentation for the children, a full contemporary band, informality and friendliness all through the service, people dressed normally, real joy and a personal welcome with eating and drinking afterwards. He was evidently impressed, almost speechless, that church could actually be, well, *good*. "It's not like the sort of church you see on the telly is it?" he said.

No it isn't. Our media's preferred projection of church is as a twee, out of touch, rather judgmental, ageing, overly formal and above all *boring* institution. That and something from the eye-bulging lunatic fringe. Virtually everything about Christianity I see on TV or hear on the radio is wildly at odds with the overwhelming majority of healthy, growing churches today. At the very least, it is a grossly unrepresentative stereotype favoured by journalists and broadcasters who can't seem to be bothered with basic research.

I have pastoral responsibility for two churches and, between them, there is a wide variety of worship styles. I happen to like *all* our services, from the more traditional, liturgical *Holy Communion* which is dignified but not stuffy, to the energetic and chaotic *Messy Church* which is accessible for and popular with families who don't do 'normal' church, to the fluid, charismatic *The Source* where spiritual gifts such as prophecy and tongues are encouraged and given full expression - and everything in between.

There are times in any of these services where Heaven seems to touch earth. These are stolen moments that cannot be artificially manufactured or prepared for. They arrive from nowhere, spontaneous instances of pure grace that make you glad to be alive and grateful that you belong to the family of God.

What do I mean by moments when Heaven touches earth? It could be to do with spiritual revelation. Recently at The Source for example, I had a word of knowledge. This is when people become aware of something that they have not learned by natural means. It's a spiritual gift (mentioned in 1 Corinthians 12.8 and shown in operation in John 4.17-18).

I felt strongly that someone in the congregation (there were perhaps 30-40 people present so it wasn't a vast crowd) had pain at the base of the back of the neck, just to the right hand side. I pointed to a very precise spot and said that if that corresponded to anyone, they should come forward for prayer. There were other words of knowledge about this time so it was no surprise to me that five or six people came forward for prayer. What did surprise me though is that not one but three people, one after another, revealed to me that they had pain in exactly the spot I had indicated.

Furthermore, I learned the following day that the woman who prayed with me for those who came forward, Sandra

Griffiths, had suffered from pain in that exact spot for about four years but decided she would not ask for prayer as three others had already been prayed for. However, when she got home that night she noticed that her pain had gone. When she woke up the next day, it was still gone and has not come back since.

The most amazing experience of this kind I have ever had was at a New Wine day on Prophecy in Versailles, France in 2003. There was a long prophetic word for me, including a revelation of my Christian name, by someone who did not know me.

The words were so accurate that my pastor at that time Anthony Wells said to me afterwards that if he had just heard an audio recording of that prophecy and somebody had asked "who do you think, of all the 6 billion people in the world, this is describing?" he would answer without hesitation that it was about me. It was slightly scary! I have since invited the man who gave that prophecy, Mark Aldridge, to speak at similar meetings and I have seen his remarkable gift of spiritual revelation overwhelm people I know well and have had pastoral responsibility for.

Other moments when Heaven has touched earth are more sacramental; a means of grace through a physical, symbolic act. I wrote about Holy Communion in the last chapter and how it uniquely seals the special bond of affection between believers. That's the horizontal aspect of the Lord's Supper. But the vertical aspect is profoundly beautiful as well.

To be honest, there are times when taking the bread and wine is as mundane an experience as it is possible to have. But there are others when eternity seems to break in to time and the soul exults in the unfathomable depths, the exquisite wonders and the holy mysteries of God's amazing grace. I have seen people unspeakably moved at the Communion rail, from quite small children to elders in their 90's.

I have at times myself become moved with emotion as I have presided at the Lord's Table. There are moments when the meekness and majesty, the sorrow and splendour and the tragedy and triumph of the cross affect me profoundly as I break the bread; "This is my body, broken for you" and lift up the cup, "This is my blood, poured out for you." It is a spiritual feast.

Other moments when Heaven has touched earth have been in musical worship. Sometimes, and it can be led by a choral group with the organ or by a contemporary band with bass guitars and drums, everybody's heart seems to be touched at once. The volume lifts unprompted. The passion rises. Or a holy stillness descends. Heads humbly bow. Hands rise upwards unselfconsciously. Smiles may appear. Tears sometimes roll down cheeks. Eyes close and people just savour the goodness of the Lord. It can be a time of unbridled exuberance. Or it can be a moment of tender intimacy.

I think that this is what David was reflecting on when he wrote these words to describe visits to the mobile temple, called the tabernacle, to worship Almighty God.

> *How priceless is your unfailing love, O God!*
> *People take refuge in the shadow of your wings.*
> *They feast in the abundance of your house;*
> *you give them drink from your river of delights.*
> *For with you is the fountain of life;*
> *in your light we see light.*
>
> Psalm 36.7-9.

Other moments when Heaven has touched earth have been in the noisy, child-friendly services for mostly unchurched families. It's called Messy Church and, at the time of writing, is one of the fastest growing forms of worship in the UK. Children can be incredibly sensitive spiritually. Actually, it doesn't have to be in church at all.

One of our most treasured "Heaven touching earth" moments was when our daughter Anna was about 2 or 3 years old. She was buckled up in the back of our old Citroen 2CV one damp, misty morning. I tried several times to start the car, but to no avail. I suppose I must have tried in vain to start the motor for about 10 minutes but, though the engine turned, it wouldn't fire. I got out and looked under the bonnet - as if someone as mechanically useless as me would know what to look for. Well who knows, there might have been something obvious like a dead badger on the carburettor. There was nothing.

I tried again, failed again, and sighed noisily, looking helpless as only men who know absolutely nothing about cars really can. Then, from the back seat, a little voice squeaked "Come on Jesus, start the car!" I hoped Anna's childlike faith would not be shattered by our useless, unreliable (French - just saying!) old banger stubbornly refusing to start yet again. But, resigned, I put the key back in the ignition. I turned the key. It started perfectly.

Other moments when Heaven has touched earth have been in preaching. Most Christians have their favourite preachers. I have mine. Some are profoundly insightful (like R. T. Kendall and David Pawson). Some are intellectually engrossing (like Tim Keller and Ravi Zacharias). Others are inspirationally fiery (such as Philippe Joret and Danielle Strickland). Some are very funny story tellers (like Eric Delve and Mike Pilavachi). Still others are passionately intense (such as C. J. Mahaney and Jackie Pullinger).

It doesn't really matter about the style; the fact is, when Heaven touches earth in preaching, the heart begins to race quicker, passion for God is stirred and faith rises up in the soul.

There is a difference between brilliant secular oratory, the sort Winston Churchill was famous for, and anointed preaching. The former can move the emotions and bolster resolve or pride over matters of life and death. The latter is the heralding of good news that not only stirs the affections, it fires up the soul. And it's much more important than mere life and death - it determines eternal destinies.

I have had many moments of Heaven touching earth as I have listened to, and engaged with, Spirit-filled, biblical preaching; times when I have had to say "I cannot go on living like I did before. I am leaving this place resolved and empowered to live a different way."

Canadian pastor and author Guy Chevreau sums up very well what I've been trying to say here. "Worship in Spirit and truth, seeing things as God sees them, attentiveness, alignment of heart, restoration and redemption, direction and revelation, may seem too much to hope for in a single service of worship. We're certainly left forever changed should we experience such holy glory."[72]

Foretastes of Heaven, usually in the context of worship, are quite unlike any other earthly experience. They are the 21st reason I am a Christian.

There's an atheist "church" that started up a few years ago in London. Weirdly, its leader has long hair and a beard and looks a bit like Jesus! It's quite popular actually. There are no prayers of course and the content is entirely secular. They sing songs, read poems or great literature, listen to a talk and meet up with each other over coffee. It sounds quite nice.

But as Oscar Wilde said, "Imitation is the sincerest form of flattery that mediocrity can pay to greatness."

I sometimes wondered if the expression "If church didn't exist, someone would have to invent it" was a slight exaggeration. But someone now has, absolutely proving the point. Some people feel they really need what church offers but, sadly, just don't believe in God.

I wonder if they experienced any of what I have described above, and I have dozens more examples I could have shared, whether they would have the courage to question their doubts. For all the enjoyment, or even inspiration, you can glean from reading Rudyard Kipling and singing The Beatles and listening to someone do a TED style talk about virtue or self-actualisation, they are hardly sublime foretastes of the eternal age to come are they?

Chapter 22

BUT DELIVER US FROM EVIL

I hesitated for a long time about including this chapter. It might raise a few eyebrows. But the truth is this: **My experiences with deliverance ministry have convinced me that evil spirits are real and that Christ is stronger.**

When I first became a Christian and read the Gospels, one of the things that stood out for me was Jesus' encounters with people troubled by evil spirits.

I had gone to a school run by Roman Catholic nuns so I grew up quite familiar with stories from the Bible. I knew all about Noah and the ark, Jonah and the fish, Daniel and the den of lions, the first Christmas and Easter, Jesus walking on water, healing lepers and feeding the 5,000 with five barley loaves and a couple of pilchards.

Maybe the Sisters of Mercy just felt that the dramatic account of a naked, self-harming man living in a graveyard, screaming uncontrollably as he met Jesus, before his many demons drove a herd of pigs off a cliff to their deaths was a bit too hardcore for primary school kids. They might have had a point actually. I can see how a lesson with all that in it could unhelpfully spring-load a class of 30 wide-eyed seven year-olds as they raced outside for morning play time!

There are 17 separate incidents of casting out evil spirits in Matthew, Mark, Luke and John, most of which are repeated at least once. The Acts of the Apostles contains 7 additional stories, besides incidental references to Christ's power over occult forces. So, as I kept coming across these accounts as a young Christian, I could see that they were not an insignificant New Testament footnote people might skate over and miss. They were in your face all over the Gospels.

As I didn't really know anything about demon possession as a young Christian, I asked others what they knew about it. One person said that they were ancient myths designed to show that good is greater than evil. (This was the man who believed the resurrection didn't really happen and that my conversion experience was an emotional high that I would probably grow out of). Others thought that talk of evil spirits was a 1st Century way of explaining some forms of mental ill health. "That was how they interpreted such things in those days" I was told. And it is certainly noticeable that the symptoms of demon possession described in some of the narratives appear very similar to an epileptic fit for example. So I was advised to think along those lines. But the people I most trusted as wise spiritual guides took the accounts at face value. The conversations would go something like this:

> "Why are there all those stories in the New Testament about people being afflicted by evil spirits?"

> "Well, they're there because sometimes people *are* afflicted by evil spirits."

> "Oh."

Ordained ministers are cautioned to be discreet about their own experiences in this realm and, true to form, I rarely speak about what I have encountered. Perhaps this is due to the fear of discrediting a respected profession in the eyes of some. It's enough already to be routinely lampooned as harmless losers in TV sitcoms without being catalogued with the likes of David Icke under "total fruitcakes and complete nutters." (Icke believes that a secret group of reptilian humanoids controls the world). This is the kind of talk that understandably gets sceptics scoffing about imaginary friends and the flying spaghetti monster.

Or perhaps this reluctance to publicise experiences of deliverance ministry is to discourage people from becoming unhealthily fascinated with the paranormal. Jesus himself of course strictly warned those he delivered from evil spirits not to speak about it afterwards to anyone.

But one of the reasons I am a Christian is down to what I have seen with my own eyes in the realm of deliverance ministry. I do not claim to be any kind of expert and I am not involved in it that often but, if you were to press them, I think the majority of church leaders would tell you that they have encountered such things at some point.

The very first time I witnessed anything of this nature was when I was in my early twenties and was at an evening service in an Anglican church in North London. As the vicar was preaching, a menacing looking man, quite well-built, entered the building, interrupted the sermon and said that he was an enemy of Christ. "My god is the god of this world. Do you know who I'm talking about?" he said. (The god of this world is a reference in the New Testament to Satan). The vicar, Owen Thomas, looked straight at him and replied "Yes, I know exactly who you're talking about and Jesus Christ is greater." The man crept off and, to my knowledge, was never seen again. Well, maybe he was just drunk. I don't know.

In 1987, Kathie and I were attending a small church plant on the south coast. About 30 people made up the church at the time. One Sunday morning, a woman in her mid-thirties became restless and agitated as people shared the Lord's Supper. She began to breathe heavily and, in an unnatural, hissing, low voice, started to express discomfort at being there. As I looked across at her, I noticed she was foaming copiously at the mouth. The elders of the church led her into an adjacent room and dealt with the situation discreetly. I don't know exactly what happened then but I guess they rebuked the spirit and ordered it to leave at once in the name of Jesus. In any case, she emerged after the service about 20 minutes later looking relaxed and at peace.

When we moved to the north-east of England my predecessor told me that at his very first service in one of my two churches he had to cast out a demon at the Communion rail. He had been ordained years before and, because he had had no experience or training in deliverance ministry, he was taught how he should go about it when he was a curate by a younger lay member of the church - which was quite humbling. He was very grateful though because it came in very useful from time to time.

I still think it's remarkable that dealing with evil spirits wasn't mentioned at all, not once, in my three years of Anglican ordination training. I am grateful that it was adequately covered at Moorlands, where I trained in cross-cultural mission 15 years earlier.

I am not going to describe every experience of deliverance ministry I have been involved in but a couple of anecdotes from the north-east particularly come to mind.

First of all, before one of our "The Source" services, as we were praying in preparation, I felt I heard the whisper of God in my soul "Tonight shall be a night of deliverance." I shared what I had sensed with those gathered with me (the service leader and musicians) but told no one else. About half an hour into the service, during a particularly powerful phase of worship, I heard behind me a slight commotion followed by a clattering of chairs. I went over to investigate and found a woman who had fallen to the floor surrounded by three or four friends. They were all visitors to my church that evening.

Asking what had happened, it became clear that the source of the incident was not something physical like vertigo or fainting; it was spiritual. The woman claimed she had been afflicted by an evil spirit for some time. Together with two church leaders from that visiting group, and in full view of those seated around them, we quietly but firmly commanded the spirit to leave her at once in the name of Jesus. Within a minute she had become calm and was able to be seated again.

Deliverance ministry such as this is quite infrequent in my experience – perhaps once every eighteen months or so on average. But this case was one of three in the space of a week. Incidents of this nature do seem to come in concentrated bursts as if the devil targets a particular season to disrupt the work of God if he can.

One of the more noteworthy instances of deliverance I have been involved in was when I had been in Stockton on Tees about six months. We received a request from a family on a nearby estate to "exorcise" a house in which there were reports of strange goings on. It was claimed that there were loud noises in the attic. Objects were being moved about in the house overnight. Things were going missing inexplicably. The children kept seeing a strangely dressed woman at night and couldn't sleep.

Three of us went to the house and asked a few questions. It turned out that the father's parents were both mediums and that there had been regular séances with a Ouija board in the house. The father, who was very welcoming and affable, would at one moment be speaking in his usual voice, but would then suddenly change tone and interrupt using foul language. When I began to read a passage of the Bible he stood straight up, came towards me and tried to tear the page out. Strangely, he had no recollection afterwards that he had been swearing or trying to damage my Bible. He was mortified when we told him. It was quite surreal.

We led the couple in a prayer of repentance, which they were very willing to say. They understood that what they had been allowing in their house had opened up the door to demonic powers. We delivered the man of his evil spirits, (if memory serves there were three), ordering them to leave in the name of Jesus. We prayed around each room of the house, including up in the attic. I understand that they went on to be part of a local church which was nearer to where they lived than ours. In any case, it seems that the problem of paranormal activity in the house was resolved at that time.

When something like that happens there is a feeling of elation when you travel home. It is amazing to see a clear demonstration of Christ's authority and power over evil forces. The 72 that Jesus sent out with his authority to preach, heal and drive out demons in Luke 10.1-20 were similarly overjoyed when they were involved in this kind of thing. "Lord, even the demons submit to us in your name." But Jesus gave a curt reply: "Do not rejoice that the spirits submit to you, but rejoice that your names are written in heaven." What did he mean?

Several times in the Bible there is a reference to a Book of Life kept by God. On one level, it sounds about as interesting as a phone directory; it just contains a list of names. It is in fact a heavenly record of every man, woman and child who has ever believed in Jesus Christ as their Saviour and bowed to Him as their Lord. According to the Bible, one day this book will be opened and those whose names are found there, whose names are "written in heaven" to use Jesus' own expression, will have the right to enjoy the eternal, inexpressibly glorious presence of God.

There's only one way you can get your name written into that book - and according to Jesus, not even casting out evil spirits makes the cut. If you've asked Jesus to be your Saviour and your Lord, your name is already written there. Jesus said to rejoice about that. Furthermore, he promised that if you belong to him, *nothing* will ever be able to remove your name from its pages. He said, "I will never blot out the name of that person from the Book of Life, but will acknowledge that name before my Father and his angels" (Revelation 3:5).

But there is also a chilling warning for those who stubbornly reject Christ's love. "If anyone's name was not found written in the book of life, he was thrown into the lake of fire" (Revelation 20:15). I hope, whatever you do, that you will not let that fate worse than death befall you. Make sure your name is written in that book. What I've experienced in the realm of deliverance, the 22nd reason I'm a Christian, persuades me that these promises and warnings are absolutely worth taking seriously.

Evil is quite real. And Jesus Christ is decisively stronger. Evil spirits *always* leave following a command to do so in his name. I know whose side I want to be on and I have settled that question. I hope you have too.

Chapter 23

SOMETHING CREEPY GOING ON

Of all my 26 reasons this is the one I think I feel most hesitant and least sure about; the phenomenon of near-death experiences. If they are genuine they show that death is not the end, that there is an afterlife and that much of what is written in the Bible about eternity is exactly right. But it's a big "if." Nevertheless this is a reason too: **Near Death Experiences suggest that death is not the end.**

According to the International Association for Near-Death Studies (IANDS) the term "near-death experience" was first coined in 1975 by Raymond Moody MD in his book *Life After Life*[73] which has gone on to sell over 13 million copies. Near Death Experiences have since become a respected field of research in medicine and psychology. The following quote is from IANDS's website.

"A near-death experience (NDE) is a distinct subjective experience that people sometimes report after a near-death episode. In a near-death episode, a person is either clinically dead, near death, or in a situation where death is likely or expected. These circumstances include serious illness or injury, such as from a car accident, military combat, childbirth, or suicide attempt. People in profound grief, in deep meditation, or just going about their normal lives have also described experiences that seem just like NDEs, even though these people were not near death. Many near-death experiencers (NDErs) have said the term 'near-death' is not correct; they are sure that they were *in* death, not just *near*-death."[74]

It is fair to say that there seems to be very little consensus in the scientific community at the present time about these experiences. Some attribute them to hallucinations. Others say they are due to an electrical surge in the dying brain. Others still refuse to take the field seriously at all, putting NDEs in roughly the same bracket as ghosts, UFOs and the conspiracy theory that the Apollo moon landings were faked. But some simply file away what is reported without any attempt to provide an explanation.

I am myself broadly sceptical but open-minded about all of this. I do not strongly believe that near-death experiences are real spiritual events. They *may* be. Truth be told, I don't actually know an awful lot about them. They could all turn out to be rationally explained by psychologists or through research into brain function. That wouldn't undo my faith in Christianity at all. It would just mean that there are 25 reasons why I think Christianity is true and not 26. But what if they *are* real?

I have only ever met one person who has claimed to have had such an experience. I cannot comment here on my perception of that person's trustworthiness. I do not know the person all that well.

There is one reason, and one reason only, why I include this in the 26 reasons and that is a curious passage in 2 Corinthians 12 in which the Apostle Paul speaks of an experience of this nature in his own life and his reluctance to make much of it.

It is not, as far as I can tell, a testimony from near death as such but as the IANDS says, "People… in deep meditation or just going about their normal lives have also described experiences that seem just like NDEs, even though these people were not near death."[75]

> This is the quote: *"I know a man in Christ who fourteen years ago was caught up to the third heaven. Whether it was in the body or out of the body I do not know - God knows. And I know that this man - whether in the body or apart from the body I do not know, but God knows - was caught up to paradise and heard inexpressible things, things that no one is*

permitted to tell. I will boast about a man like that, but I will not boast about myself, except about my weaknesses. Even if I should choose to boast, I would not be a fool, because I would be speaking the truth. But I refrain, so no one will think more of me than is warranted by what I do or say, or because of these surpassingly great revelations."

2 Corinthians 12.2-7.

Paul says here that someone he knew (it might have been an indirect way of speaking of himself as the end of the quotation possibly indicates) had a vivid experience of some heavenly place -perhaps physically, perhaps in a trance-like state- and that it was completely indescribable.

I keep an open mind about what people say has happened to them, especially I must say when it's rewarded with a publishing contract, but I believe the Bible is trustworthy and true. I consider the testimony of an Apostle writing Scripture under the inspiration of the Holy Spirit to have weight. That's my starting point. I do not write off all these stories out of hand when there is one such testimony in the Bible. I have tentatively come to believe that God might well sometimes give departing believers glimpses of what is to come partly perhaps to encourage us who remain.

The evangelist Billy Graham once said, "Just before dying, my grandmother sat up in bed, smiled, saying 'I see Jesus and he has his hand outstretched to me. And there is Ben and he has both of his eyes and both of his legs.'" (Ben, Billy Graham's grandfather, had lost an eye and a leg in war).[76] Sceptics might say of course that this is just delirium or wishful thinking. I do not say categorically that they are wrong. They may indeed be right. But I don't know... There are several books out at the moment by people who claim to have had foretastes of heaven during a serious illness only to make a full recovery. I think these testimonies deserve to be heard without prejudice.

One recent book I found particularly interesting is called *Heaven Is For Real* by Todd Burpo about his four-year old son Colton (Colton Burpo - what an unusual name!) in which the child had undergone life-threatening surgery following a burst appendix. Thankfully, Colton survived the operation.

But following the surgery, it became apparent that the child had had a remarkable and mystifying experience while still on the operating table. Days, weeks, even months following the operation Colton would talk unprompted, and matter-of-factly about being able to look down and watch the medical staff perform the surgery and see his father desperately praying in an adjacent room. His description of the scene in the waiting room was exactly correct, even though the young boy had at no time actually been there.

Other details slowly emerged as, now and again, Colton would come out with "what he had seen in heaven." He said for example that he had met his miscarried sister, about whom he had no prior knowledge. He described meeting with his great grandfather, portraying him accurately, and who had died years before Colton was born. He gave full and exact descriptions, in child's language, of obscure details in the Bible - things he would not have learned in Sunday school or heard at home. That is just a short summary. There's a lot more in the book.

Unless Colton's pastor father is an absolute charlatan who has manipulated his pre-school aged son to defend an elaborate lie as he grows up, it is hard to explain this away. Certainly, it doesn't fit as some kind of trick of the mind when in trauma.

Another interesting testimony is from the Harvard trained neurosurgeon Dr. Eben Alexander. The Huffington Post carried an article about him and it is as balanced as you would expect from such a respected, secular source.[77] This testimony is particularly thought-provoking because Dr. Alexander had, until his own NDE in the autumn of 2008, been highly sceptical of such phenomena. He was of the view that NDEs *feel* real, but are no more than fantasies produced by the brain when under extreme stress. Then, Dr. Alexander suffered a rare illness, bacterial meningitis. The part of the brain that commands thought and emotion completely shut down. Alexander lay in a coma for a full week. Then, as his doctors considered discontinuing treatment, his eyes suddenly opened. He then began to speak of what he had experienced while in his comatose state.

Dr. Raymond Moody whom I referenced above as the person who first coined the expression "near-death experiences" has gone on record about Dr. Alexander's story saying "Dr. Eben Alexander's near-death experience is the most astounding I have heard in more than four decades of studying this phenomenon... one of the crown jewels of all near death experiences... Dr. Alexander is living proof of an afterlife."[78]

Now again, it may be that this man is making it all up in order to sell books. He certainly has done that, topping the New York Times bestsellers list. But if that is the case, he has completely hoodwinked one of the world's leading academic authorities on the subject, risking his entire career and professional reputation as he did. Or he may simply be mistaken or deluded. In fairness, Alexander has attracted strong opposition from critics who have attempted to explain his experiences in purely natural terms. He has publicly refuted each attack, defending his account vigorously.

But there are many, many other stories of near-death experiences. Many of them confirm biblical teaching. Some of them are more esoteric and new-age in feel – which in my view is the biggest argument against their authenticity.

Nevertheless, though I find all this quite interesting, my belief in life after death is not based on anecdotes and testimonies of this nature. My faith in heaven, hell and eternal life is founded on the well-attested historical fact of the resurrection of Jesus Christ from the dead, which I put forward in chapter 14.

Everyone knows that if science finds a rational explanation for NDEs it will merely mean that there's a rational explanation for NDEs. No big deal. But what if it doesn't? What if these experiences *are* based on a spiritual reality we cannot explain and *not* on the imagination or some malfunction of the brain when it shuts down? Then there is a big deal. While the research goes on, I read stories like those quoted above with a detached curiosity. And until good evidence is produced to prove the contrary, NDEs lend some modest supporting testimony to my belief that heaven is real and they furnish me with a 23rd reason for being a Christian.

Chapter 24

THE GREAT UNKNOWN

I am now drawing near to the end of trying to say why I am a Christian and why I think people should reconsider before dismissing it out of hand.

As I said at the start, I don't think that any one reason, on its own, would be enough for me to believe that Christianity must be true. The one that probably gets closest is the one about the resurrection (chapter 14) but even that one leaves a nagging "what if…" especially when something truly awful happens where even the most convinced believer briefly wonders if life isn't just a roulette wheel of good and bad luck.

But taken together, the 23 reasons so far make up a cumulative case built on what I think and what I have experienced. As a whole, what I have tried to say up till now satisfies me that I am not deluded or brain-dead and that Christianity really is true. Basically, it all adds up for me and I think if you have read honestly, with an open mind, at all I have written so far you would have to admit that the case for Christianity is a serious one even if you still aren't personally convinced.

If I wasn't a Christian I would be something else. I have wondered about the "something elses" for a long time and these last three chapters are about why I do not go along with the three most popular alternatives to being a Christian; religion, atheism and agnosticism.

What about other religions? Could it be that I am just naturally credulous? Do I just need to believe in something as a crutch to help me limp through life? If so, might I have joined another religion had I not become a Christian? What if I was attracted to being a Christian simply because I was born in Britain? What if I had been born in Japan or India or Saudi Arabia or Thailand? Would I have become a Shintoist, a Hindu, a Muslim or a Buddhist?

Or what about atheism? What if all I had ever read about religion was a cascade of put downs, trolling and generalisations on Internet forums? Would I never have taken Christianity seriously at all? If I had been brought up by atheist parents, self-named 'brights' who scoffed at Christian faith and suppressed any interest in spiritual things throughout my childhood, would I have ended up an atheist like them? Maybe. But I've thought about atheism, I've read their stuff, I've dialogued with some of them - and decided that atheism too misses the mark.

But this chapter is about agnosticism. I have thought it through carefully and decided that I am not going to be an agnostic. **Agnostics sound fair-minded and reasonable but I just can't be one.**

There is a small core of people who self-identify as believers whether they are Christians, Hindus, Muslims, Jews or whatever. They tend to get ribbed at school. Well, not so much the Hindus, Muslims, Jews etc., because that might be seen as racist or islamophobic or anti-Semitic or intolerant. Then there is a growing and vocal core of people who self-identify as atheists. They are never picked on at school unless they are overweight, or ginger, or have zits, or wear the wrong trainers, or like the wrong music. But not because they proclaim that there is no god - no one gives anyone a hard time for that.

But the majority of people in the UK are pretty live-and-let-live about such things. Probably most of the population in the UK - I would hazard a guess that about 60-70% - is agnostic. "Yes there might be a God, probably not in all honesty, but who can really say for sure? Churches don't seem to do too much harm, a few obvious bad apples apart; they even do quite a lot of good, and if you're that way inclined, going along might help you. But it's not for me." This is probably the default world view of the majority of people in the U.K.

Many such people don't think very much about spiritual things. They just don't feel the need to, although in times of need most will not hesitate to send up a quick prayer just in case. "If there's a God – fine. If not, well, whatever."

If you asked the question for a survey in the U.K., "Is there a God?"

- ☐ Yes
- ☐ No
- ☐ Don't know

most, I guess, would tick box number 3. These are the agnostics.

In a way, I really respect agnostics. Generally, they are not heavy or antagonistic. They don't wait like a coiled spring, ready to react the moment someone expresses an opinion consistent with the Bible. They don't go around saying that they're scientifically right and everyone who thinks differently to them is brain-dead. There's a refreshing intellectual honesty about agnostics. "You might be right. You might be wrong. Whichever way round it is, let's agree to get on and not attack each other." I like that. I never feel that agnostics are trying to convert me to their way of thinking or indeed scold me for mine.

I warm to people who, when I ask them a question, reply "I honestly don't know" instead of bluffing and pretending they do.

The comedian David Mitchell (who was brought up in a Jewish home) in a YouTube clip has recently admitted to being an agnostic and, unlike many vocal fellow TV personalities, not an atheist. This is part of his interview:

> "I don't accept the argument that atheism is the most rational response to the world as we see it. I think agnosticism is. And I don't want there to be nothing. No, I'm not convinced there's something but I do want there to be something. I want there to be an all-powerful, benevolent God and I like that thought. And I was initially brought up with it and now I'm not sure – but I'm not ready to reject it and I'm suspicious of the disdain for people who find that a comfort in their lives."

What could be fairer than that? David Mitchell's approach appeals because it is eminently reasonable and fair-minded and tolerant of difference. It is open to discussion and persuasion. It is not that brand of agnosticism that says that we *can't* know if there is a God or not so don't bother looking. Mitchell just says he doesn't know; he's honestly not convinced as things stand, but he sees no virtue in being completely closed about it.

If I wasn't a Christian I would probably be an agnostic. After all, it's what I was before I was a Christian.

And yet in some ways an agnostic is the worst possible thing to be. You see, either my name is Derek or it isn't. There is no perhaps. Either you are married or you're single. There is no maybe. You are a smoker or you don't smoke. In the same way, either there is a God or there isn't.

So it might just be that atheists have been right all along. Perhaps there is no god after all. Maybe it is just a silly fantasy or dangerous figment of people's imagination and people like Sam Harris and Christopher Hitchens have validly made a fortune selling books saying so because they are correct in their assertion that "God" is a hare-brained and toxic delusion.

Or on the other hand, it may be that theists are right instead. Perhaps there really *is* a God who made the universe and is behind our concepts of virtue, truth, justice and beauty. Maybe it's true.

The Irish poet W.B. Yeats is said to have summed up the fatal weakness in the agnostic position when he said, somewhat tongue in cheek, "Some people say there is a God. Others say there is no God. The truth probably lies somewhere in between!" Of course the truth is not in between, but at one of the poles. Either there is a God or there isn't. But whichever it is, agnostics are wrong.

Put it another way. Anyone can back the wrong horse. At the racecourse, most people do in fact; and that explains why the guy who runs the betting shop might drive a top-of-the-range car. But in a two-horse race, what is the point in backing neither runner because you really can't choose between them? Either way, you miss out on the winnings.

Stephen Gaukroger in his little book *It Makes Sense* asks you to imagine that you are about to drown at sea. You've just had a third lungful of sea water and it's not looking good. As it happens, you know that there are two boats nearby. One will get you home safe and dry. The other is packed with explosives ready to go off at any moment. If you're an agnostic, Gaukroger says, you choose to stay in the water. One boat heads back to port. The other is blown to smithereens. *And you drown.* You were absolutely right about the perilous danger of one of those boats – but absolutely wrong to stay in the sea.[79] Rejecting both the reality of God and the unreality of God, agnostics are condemned to make the wrong choice because either God exists or he doesn't. Agnosticism is therefore the worst of all worlds.

About 3,500 years ago Moses spoke to the whole Israelite nation in these words:

> *This day I call the heavens and the earth as witnesses against you that I have set before you life and death,*

blessings and curses. Now choose life, so that you and your children may live and that you may love the Lord your God, listen to his voice, and hold fast to him. For the Lord is your life, and he will give you many years in the land he swore to give to your fathers, Abraham, Isaac and Jacob.

Deuteronomy 30.19-20.

He was saying "Come on, make your mind up. Don't sit on the fence forever." That's why I am not an agnostic any more. When I left the safety of my uncertainties and discovered the sure riches of Jesus Christ I knew there was no going back. I absolutely don't regret it and never have. That's the 24th reason I am a Christian.

Chapter 25

MUCH ADO ABOUT NOTHING

I'm not an atheist because, apart from the fact that I believe that there is a God, I also think atheism offers nothing, transforms no one and leads nowhere.

In respect to the question of God, if agnostics are probably the biggest group in the UK, then atheists are surely the most vocal. Indeed the BBC journalist John Humphrys noted that, of all the people he met in the production of his acclaimed 2006 television series *Humphrys In Search Of God*, the atheists were quite the most dogmatic and opinionated.

Of course, every sane man, woman and child would agree that twenty Muslim fanatics hijacking airliners and flying them into buildings is an appalling and unprecedented outrage. But the wave of anger those 2001 attacks provoked gave birth to a mood among many since then that has tarred the likes of good Christian people like Desmond Tutu, Billy Graham, Mother Teresa and Martin Luther King with the same brush.

In the decade following that atrocity in the USA there was a spate of books published that discredited religious faith *of any kind* and attacked it as derisible, delusional and dangerous. Richard Dawkins' *The God Delusion*, Christopher Hitchens' *God Is Not Great*, Sam Harris' *The End of Faith* and Daniel Dennett's *Breaking the Spell* are perhaps the best known and have become hugely influential.[80] These books, arriving on the market more or less simultaneously, gave rise to the expression "the new atheism".

This atheism was not a cautious or inhibited version, content to not believe in God and beg to differ with those who do. Before 9/11, I felt that most atheists regarded my faith as more or less inoffensive - if misguided. A bit annoying at worst. But the tone of the new atheism is argumentative and condescending. It considers *all* religious belief as humankind's most evil enemy and feels driven to eradicate it. To me, this feels like a campaign to permanently ban football because of the occasional incidence of hooliganism. Such is the contempt for religious faith that the notion of parents passing on their Christian values and beliefs to their children was condemned in *The God Delusion* as worse than child sexual abuse. Yes, *worse*.

In a way, there is nothing new about this "new" atheism. It mirrors the anticlerical backlash in the 18th Century that led to the French Revolution; an essentially atheist uprising. The famous slogan "Men will never be free until the last king is strangled with the entrails of the last priest" was attributed to Denis Diderot. He died shortly before the Revolution but his passionate oratory was one of the driving forces behind it.

In more recent times, the dogma of the Communist Party in East Germany used similar rhetoric. The Stasi's programme of certifying church pastors amongst others as insane and subjecting them to forced labour or mental health institutions or summary execution was powered by a conviction that upholding Christian values and beliefs is bad for society and must be stamped out at any cost. Children were forcibly removed from their Christian parents and indoctrinated against them. Now *that* surely is a crime comparable to child sexual abuse.

Of course, none of the new atheists mentioned above would advocate cruelty such as the examples I have just cited and I am not seeking to begrime their reputations by suggesting that they would. But their ideas, and the tone in which they are expressed, are an ideological pestilence when fed to the minds of people with total political control such as Josef Stalin, Pol Pot, Nicolai Ceausescu, Mao Zedong and Kim Jong Un. This is a point the new atheists fail to concede to their shame. Richard Dawkins displays his naivety when he writes in *The God Delusion* "I do not believe there is an atheist in the world who would bulldoze Mecca – or Chartres, York Minster or Notre Dame."[81] But Professor Dawkins' undoubted expertise in the field of biology does not extend to his having even the most basic grasp of history - as the people of East Germany and North Korea among many others would readily attest. They would tell him for example of how their proudly atheist states dynamited the Paulinerkirche in Leipzig and bulldozed churches in Pyongyang to make way for their irreligious monuments.

But if only it were just a matter of razing the odd church building to the ground. Alas, so unvaryingly appalling is the track record of institutionalized atheism on the lives of those who dissent from it that Christopher Hitchens, for example, has sought to wriggle out of the embarrassment by suggesting that the atheism that spawned the Soviet Gulag, the Cambodian Killing Fields and the Chinese Cultural Revolution Purges is not really atheist at all but essentially *religious* in nature. This silly denial is as laughable as claiming that the 9/11 terrorists were not really radicalised Muslims, but Jedi knights who had turned to the Dark Side.

One of the tactics of the new atheists is to compare and contrast the best of moderate atheism with the worst of extremist religion and say "Look how awful religion always is compared to rational, peace-loving, tolerant, educated atheism!" The truth is of course that there is fundamentalist, extremist religion and there is fundamentalist, extremist atheism. Give either enough power and they will both tend to exterminate dissenters in equal measure and with similar unconcern, convinced they doing humanity a favour. Then there is tolerant, moderate religion and tolerant, moderate atheism. Both are usually basically civilised and humanitarian, though I would argue that far more good in the world is done in the name of Christ than for any other cause.

Atheist journalist Matthew Parris wrote a now famous piece in *The Times* in 2008 in which he had the courage to admit that Christianity, not atheism, has been a greater force for good in Africa than anything else. Here is a short extract, edited for the sake of brevity:

> "Now a confirmed atheist, I've become convinced of the enormous contribution that Christian evangelism makes in Africa: sharply distinct from the work of secular NGOs, government projects and international aid efforts... In Africa Christianity changes people's hearts. It brings a spiritual transformation. The rebirth is real. The change is good... It's a pity, I would say, that salvation is part of the package, but Christians black and white, working in Africa, do heal the sick, do teach people to read and write; and only the severest kind of

secularist could see a mission hospital or school and say the world would be better without it. I would allow that if faith was needed to motivate missionaries to help, then, fine: but what counted was the help, not the faith. But this doesn't fit the facts. Faith does more than support the missionary; it is also transferred to his flock... We had friends who were missionaries, and as a child I stayed often with them; I also stayed, alone with my little brother, in a traditional rural African village. In the city we had working for us Africans who had converted and were strong believers. The Christians were always different. Far from having cowed or confined its converts, their faith appeared to have liberated and relaxed them. There was a liveliness, a curiosity, an engagement with the world - a directness in their dealings with others - that seemed to be missing in traditional African life. They stood tall."[82]

Is this Christianity the driving force that, in the words of Christopher Hitchens, "poisons everything"? To slightly misquote Shakespeare, the gentleman doth protest too much, methinks.

The opposite charge could just as easily be made - that it is *atheism* that poisons everything precisely because of its absolute refusal of any accountability to a higher authority.

Polish Nobel laureate Czeslaw Milosz (1911-2004) suffered at the hands of both the Nazis and the Soviets and made the point that it was atheism, not religious belief, that made those regimes as insatiably murderous as they were. In *The Discreet Charm of Nihilism* he wrote "A true opium of the people is a belief in nothingness after death, the huge solace of thinking that for our betrayals, greed, cowardice, murders we are not going to be judged. The Marxist creed has been inverted. The true opium of modernity is the belief that there is *no* God, so that humans are free to do precisely as they please."[83]

Nor do I agree that atheism is a new, enlightened, grown up way of thinking, which has left the childish era of belief behind in the dark ages. This is a widely held view in the West today. I contend that it is false. Atheism is not new at all. The Epicurean philosophers who lived around 300 years before Christ had a strictly materialist view of the world and rejected any notion of divine intervention including creation insisting that matter had always existed and that life came and went entirely through natural processes. They too came and went. 1,000 years before Christ the Bible twice declared: "Fools say in their hearts that there is no God" (Psalm 14.1 and Psalm 53.1).

I reject atheism because I dissent from its central assertion that there is no God. But I also reject atheism because it offers nothing, transforms no one and leads nowhere.

It offers nothing. Atheism is simply a belief that there is no God. The God revealed in Jesus Christ offers spiritual salvation, unspeakable joy, profound peace, healed relationships, new purpose, transformative forgiveness, real community, eternal life and more. But atheism denies that there is a God, so it forbids its adherents all of what God freely gives. Atheism offers *nothing*.

It transforms no one. I know former drug addicts who were delivered from their addiction when they converted to Christ. I know former serial offenders who became responsible husbands and fathers earning an honest wage after they became Christians. I know former cranky, vain, self-absorbed people who became givers with a love for the poor when they encountered Jesus. But I do not meet atheists with a *testimony*. Yes, I know atheists who used to be believers and lost their faith. But I never hear anyone say "I used to be a born-again Christian and my life was empty. I had no sense of purpose. But then, oh happy day, I became an atheist and my life has changed. I am now so full of joy. I finally know where I'm going in life and I have started to serve hot meals to homeless people in the town centre every Saturday." I'm not holding my breath. Atheism transforms *no one*.

And it leads nowhere. Atheism is a protest movement that fails to deliver any credible alternative. The nearest atheism gets to offering something positive instead of just attacking something else is the well-publicised London public transport advert campaign in 2009. Buses carried adverts with the slogan "There's probably no God. Now stop worrying and enjoy your life." But I don't know any worried, anxious Christians whose miserable lives would suddenly get better by ceasing to go to church and pray. Who was this silly campaign aimed at? It cost £140,000. Wouldn't the money have been better spent providing safe drinking water for hundreds of villages in Africa? Obviously. But atheism has very little energy in it for making the world a better place for the poor – it leads *nowhere*.

As Francis Spufford wrote in the extended rant to atheists that is his book *Unapologetic*: "For many of you, the point of atheism appears to be not the non-relationship with God but a live and hostile relationship with believers. It isn't enough that you yourselves don't believe: atheism permits a delicious self-righteous anger at those who do. The very existence of religion seems to be an affront, a liberty being taken, a scab you can't help picking. People who don't like stamp-collecting don't have a special magazine called The Anti-Philatelist. But you do… It's as if there is some transgressive little ripple of satisfaction which can only be obtained by uttering the words 'sky fairy' or 'zombie rabbi' where a real live Christian might hear them."[84] I am not sure I like Spufford's tone if I'm honest but I do share the exasperation.

I have thought about it long and hard and found that, not only is atheism profoundly mistaken on the existence of God, I agree with Matthew Parris; it just doesn't *deliver*.

Here's the sort of thing I mean by "deliver." Kirsten Powers is a political commentator with Fox News. A few years ago, she was an avowed atheist who held evangelical Christianity in particular contempt. But now she is... an evangelical Christian. This is part of her story.

"When I moved to New York, where I worked in Democratic politics, my world became aggressively secular. Everyone I knew was politically left-leaning, and my group of friends was overwhelmingly atheist... I derided Christians as anti-intellectual bigots who were too weak to face the reality that there is no rhyme or reason to the world."

She started dating a Christian boyfriend who invited her to his church in Manhattan led by Tim Keller, She went along.

"Each week, Keller made the case for Christianity. He also made the case against atheism and agnosticism. He expertly exposed the intellectual weaknesses of a purely secular worldview. I came to realize that even if Christianity wasn't the real thing, neither was atheism."

After some time and following a strange but vivid dream about Jesus she agreed to attend a midweek discussion group.

"I had a knot in my stomach. In my mind, only weirdoes and zealots went to Bible studies. I don't remember what was said that day. All I know is that when I left, everything had changed. I'll never forget standing outside that apartment on the Upper East Side and saying to myself, 'It's true. It's completely true.' The world looked entirely different, like a veil had been lifted off it. I had not an iota of doubt. I was filled with indescribable joy."[85]

People often think that Christians are conformists who have denied themselves the liberty of independent thought. In fact, it's anything but. Becoming a Christian is not a smart career move for those in the media. It takes real courage in an environment like Kirsten's, and many others, to step out from the security of her peer group and risk criticism and contempt.

No matter. "Indescribable joy" she said. *That's what I felt* when I became a Christian in 1979. I still have flashes of it now through Christian friendships, in prayer and worship, even in times of pain and loss. "It's true. It's completely true" she said. *That's what I thought* the day I gave my life to Christ. I still think it is. Some days it seems so obviously true that I wonder how anyone could arrive at any other conclusion. "The world looked entirely different" she said. That is not so much my experience, but I have heard many Christians say exactly that about their conversion. The world actually looks physically different. Kirsten Powers' story, and thousands like it, are one of several reasons why I am not an atheist and one of 26 why I am a Christian.

Chapter 26

IMAGINE NO RELIGION

The Christmas that followed my conversion in the summer of 1979, my sister offered me a book called *The Lion Handbook of the World's Religions*. Written inside the front cover was a short message saying "…because you can never be too sure if you've chosen the right one." I still have the book on my shelf.

It was thoughtful of her to offer me that gift and the fact I still have it is testament to how useful it has proved over the years. How many Christmas presents have you received in your life that you still have three and a half decades later? But, that said, I think my sister's little note betrays a fateful error in the way people usually think of Christianity.

You see, not one religion attracts me at all. **I have absolutely no interest whatsoever in belonging to a religion.** I never have done. It might seem weird to some, as I have been a Christian for over 35 years but I have never once considered myself "religious." I have been a pioneer missionary and church leader since 1990 and yet I have to quickly correct people when they say I like religion. I really *don't*. I am not at all a religious person. It doesn't attract me or interest me. Yes, I pray regularly, read the Bible and believe its message is trustworthy. But there is a vast chasm between adhering to a religion and belonging to Jesus Christ.

The Christian stand-up comedian Milton Jones put it really well: "To say that Christianity is just one of several religions is a bit like saying that water is just one of many types of drink - it's a bit more fundamental than that."

Religion is about the ways people try to reach God. There are many of them. A relationship with Jesus Christ is about the way God has reached people. It is unique. Religion is about people trying hard to become acceptable to God. A relationship with Jesus Christ is about how, through faith, God has already made us pleasing to him. Religion is about performance and good works and trying harder. A relationship with Jesus Christ is about conceding that his good work on the cross is enough. Religion says "I am a good person." A relationship with Jesus Christ says "Lord, change me because I am not a good person." Religion repeats dutiful rituals, pious observances and correct procedures. In a relationship with Jesus Christ all that just gets in the way.

It might surprise people to hear that God doesn't like religion either. This is what he says in the Old Testament:

> *Stop bringing meaningless offerings!*
> *Your incense is detestable to me...*
> *I cannot bear your worthless assemblies.*
>
> Isaiah 1.13.

Ah yes, even *God* really can't stand ritualistic religion because it tends to blind people to the simple truth about Jesus Christ. It doesn't help people who are weighed down by addictions or imprisoned by destructive feelings. Religion doesn't change hearts. If anything it tends to harden them.

The New Testament rejection of religion is just as uncompromising.

> *Do not let anyone judge you by what you eat or drink, or with regard to a religious festival, a New Moon celebration or a Sabbath day. These are a shadow of the things that were to come; the reality, however, is found in Christ... Why, as though you still belonged to the world, do you submit to its rules: 'Do not handle! Do not taste! Do not touch!'? These rules, which have to do with things that are all destined to perish with use, are based on merely human commands and teachings. Such regulations indeed have an appearance of wisdom, with their self-imposed worship, their false humility and*

their harsh treatment of the body, but they lack any value in restraining sensual indulgence.
From Colossians 2.16-23.

Sadly, Christians often drift away from the straightforward unfussiness of a relationship with God through Jesus Christ to spending a small fortune on worthless accessories - 'Jesus tat' I call it. Yuck! There is so much otherworldly religiosity around. It all leaves me cold.

Religion says, "you have got to bathe in this particular river." It says "you mustn't eat this or that food or drink any alcohol." It says "you've got to fast for a month." It says "you males have to be circumcised." It says "you mustn't cut your hair." It says "you *must* cut your hair." It says "you've got to face a certain direction to pray." It says "wear a turban," "wear a skull cap", "don't wear shoes here", "wear an orange robe," "wear a full-length black garment that covers everything but your eyes." But Jesus came and said, "Love God and love other people as you love yourself." That's about it. I mean no disrespect to those who like religion. I just think Jesus' approach is much better.

But is there nothing at all about the religious life that might be useful in any way? Can people not be good Sikhs, Hindus, Jews, Buddhists and Muslims? Of course! Like everyone else, I know people who are devout believers from other religious communities. They live upright lives, bring up their children well, are at peace and give something back to society.

I am not so naive or narrow-minded to imagine that all non-Christian religions and sects have nothing good about them at all. No, I agree with Sikhs that sin is real and serious. I agree with Hindus that marriage is a life-giving and life-long covenant between one man and one woman. I agree with Jews that God created the heavens and the earth. I agree with Buddhists that indulging in pleasure is never the route to true fulfilment. I agree with Muslims that God will one day judge the living and the dead.

There is some truth in all religions; otherwise I don't think anyone would be dumb enough to follow them. So I honour all that is valuable in religion. I make it my aim to get along with everyone and see the good in them. But I don't think all the religious practices and rituals and observances and duties and icons and trinkets and rules can ever make God more accessible. I think *Jesus* makes God more accessible.

I haven't got space here to critique each religion and explain why I have rejected each one. I could, for example, write about how Hinduism has not only failed to challenge the unjust caste system but is in fact responsible for it. I could also write about why I think Islam will always have a violent, extremist branch within it. And so on and so on. But the bottom line is that I know that it will look highly selective and I freely admit that organised Christianity has had many failings too. (In my view though, unlike with other religions, the Church goes wrong when its members *deviate from* the teachings of its founder).

What I want to do instead is end this book by looking at Jesus again. Many other religions think well of Jesus. But none, not one, worships him as God incarnate or proclaims him Lord of lords – except Christianity. That's the problem. I don't want to be an adherent of any movement that declines to afford Jesus admiration in proportion to his greatness.

In the James Stewart film *It's a Wonderful Life* the main character gets to see what his town would have been like if he had never been born. What I know is that our world would be much worse if Jesus had never been born. This thought might come as something of a surprise to many because it seems that whenever the merits or otherwise of Christianity are debated on the radio or TV, someone says that religion just leads to more hatred and war. I'm amazed at how few people challenge this.

If the First and Second World Wars had been started by the Pope and the Archbishop of Canterbury over some trifle of doctrine I'd sympathize with the outrage against the Church. There weren't of course; they were both caused by the exaltation of the nation-state. The fact is that the world was torn apart many times by wars before Jesus was born. Most wars fought since he was born had nothing whatever to do with him. The one blot on the landscape, the Crusades 800 years ago, were waged in direct defiance of Jesus' own teaching to "love your enemies."

If Jesus had never been born, there would be no AD after the year because AD means the Year of our Lord.

Places we know as El Salvador, St. Albans, St. Petersburg, Sao Paolo, San Francisco, Christchurch, Corpus Christi, Santa Cruz, Asunción and Bishop Auckland would all have a different name.

Everybody you know called Christine, Christian, Christelle or Christopher would have been named something else.

Many idioms would never have entered our every day speech; Good Samaritan, prodigal son, wolf in sheep's clothing, love your neighbour, go the second mile, do to others as you would have them do to you, turn the other cheek and salt of the earth; to name only a few were all coined by Jesus.

We would never have heard of Santa Claus. The fat, bearded chap in a red velvet suit from the North Pole is based on a real person; a generous Christian bishop from Turkey who gave dowries to impoverished girls so that they would not have to become prostitutes.

We would never have heard "Amazing Grace", "Oh Happy Day!", Handel's "Halleluiah Chorus" or "Hark the Herald Angels Sing."

We might have never heard of Martin Luther King or Mother Teresa. Blacks in America might still be second class citizens and the poor of Calcutta would still have no one to love them.

Organizations such as the Samaritans, Christian Aid, the Red Cross and the Salvation Army would not have been founded. Life for the suicidal, the sick, the hungry and the world's poor would probably be much, much worse.

The first free hospital, 1,700 years before the NHS and 1,770 years before "Obamacare", would never have been built – and nor would tens of thousands after it.

The slave trade might still be here, since it was opposed almost single-handedly on biblical principles by a Christian politician - William Wilberforce.

Thousands of schools around the world would never have opened their doors, including all church schools in Britain today, most of them with long waiting lists and for good reason.

Oxford, Cambridge, Paris Sorbonne, Princeton, Harvard and Yale Universities would not have been founded.

We wouldn't have much priceless classical art including Michelangelo's Sistine Chapel ceiling.

We would have no films such as *It's a Wonderful Life*, *Ben Hur*, *Chariots of Fire*, *The Lion the Witch and the Wardrobe*, and scores of others.

We would have no Shakespeare's *Measure for Measure*, no Dickens's *Christmas Carol*, and no Victor Hugo's *Les Misérables*.

The United Kingdom would never have had a national anthem which addresses God and asks him to save; it would probably be a pagan nation worshipping the sun and the moon as fertility symbols.

The flags of Denmark, England, Finland, Greece, Iceland, Norway, Scotland, Sweden and Switzerland would not have a cross on them.

We would never swear on the Bible in court or say that anything is "gospel truth."

The net flow of immigration in the world today would not be from non-Christian countries to "Christianised" ones – because they would probably not be more desirable places to live.

The Auca Indians of Ecuador would still be spearing white men to death instead of baptizing their children.

The Arawakan natives of the Caribbean would still be cannibals. Descendants of the Maya in Mexico would still sacrifice their children instead of teaching them to praise their Creator.

If Jesus had never been born, hundreds of Old Testament prophecies would have remained unfulfilled. Death would not have been conquered. God would be a liar.

There would be no mediator between God and man, for the only one able to bring God and man together, Jesus, would have been as fictitious as the tooth fairy, morbidly obese men getting down chimneys or flying reindeer. We would still have no hope of eternal life.

What a difference Jesus makes! No other religious figure comes close to impacting the world for good like he has. No other religion recognises him as the Saviour of the world. That's why none of them can ever capture my heart - and it's the 26th and ultimate reason why I am a Christian.

Footnote

BELIEVE IT OR NOT

So there we have it. 26 reasons why I believe I am not wasting my life by being a Christian, and am not forgoing a worthwhile career path by becoming a church leader.

Perhaps in hindsight I could have chosen others. Perhaps a chapter on all the prayers I have seen answered, sometimes in the most extraordinary way. But I would have to acknowledge that some of my prayers are yet unanswered. Suffice to say that, as the former Archbishop of Canterbury William Temple who in reply to criticism that answered prayer was just coincidence said, "When I pray, coincidences happen; when I don't, they don't."

Perhaps I could have written a chapter on healing as well as deliverance. I have personally witnessed people being healed from many ailments from migraines to skin rashes to tinnitus to depression to stammers to various aches and pains. I have a friend who has seen people instantly healed of blindness, deafness, irregular heartbeat and advanced cancer witnessed by crowds and verified by a medical doctor. But equally, I have seen people prayed for time and time again with little or no improvement to their condition. All I know is that when people pray for healing in Jesus' name more people get healed than when no one prays for healing in Jesus' name.

But I have stuck with the 26 I jotted down at the end of 2012. We'll leave it there.

I *love* being a Christian. Every year I have new surprises and experience new aspects of the unsurpassed excellence of Jesus Christ.

I *love* being a church leader too. In 2014, The Office for National Statistics compiled a report on job satisfaction. They compared 274 different careers and occupations. You might think that pub landlord might be quite high up the list – what could be more satisfying than getting paid for pulling pints and chatting in bars all week? You might also hazard a guess that vicar might be quite low down the scale. Like Father McKenzie in the Beatles' *Eleanor Rigby*, what more discouraging and useless career can you imagine that presiding over dwindling, ageing congregations and burying the dead at funerals no one attends? In fact, vicar was the number one occupation for job satisfaction and pub landlord was 274th – rock bottom.[86] The *Eleanor Rigby* caricature portrayed by many sections of the media of a Church that is absolutely dire is misleading. Some such churches are in decline. They've had their day. But the vast majority of growing churches are bursting with life. They are youthful and vibrant. They have good news stories to tell. They are absolutely why vicar is the most satisfying occupation of all.

I can't remember if Rock Star or Author were on the list of occupations for job satisfaction. But consider the following two paragraphs.

The Rolling Stones in the 1960s went overboard on sex, drugs and rock and roll - they are still famous for it now. They are millionaires living in mansions with swimming pools, driving Bentleys and are adored by fans all over the world - but their most iconic song is not called "I'm Living the Dream, Baby." It's called "I Can't Get No Satisfaction."

The millionaire writer Jack Higgins has penned over 80 novels including the classic *The Eagle Has Landed*. They have sold over 150 million copies and been translated into 55 languages. He was once asked on the radio what he knew today that he would like to have known as a boy. He thought for a moment. Then he said, "I wish I had known then what I know now - that when you get to the top, there's nothing there."

I wouldn't mind getting to the top myself just to see personally if there really *is* nothing up there! If you want to check it out for yourself, keep climbing.

In the meantime, thanks for taking the time out to read this. If you started out as a believer, I hope this has helped to make your faith stronger. If your mind was made up that Christianity is rubbish before you started, it probably hasn't made any difference but I am glad that you made it to the end without throwing the book in the recycling. I hope you've at least found it thought-provoking and that we can be friends. If you began sceptical but with an open mind I wonder if anything has changed. What if there really is more to life than what you have so far experienced? What if there is a spiritual side to life that nothing this world affords can satisfy? Over to you to make the next step. Safe journeys.

NOTES

1. During an address at the Faith Angle Forum, November 3-5 2013 in South Beach, Florida, USA.
2. Lennox, John D., *God's Undertaker*, Oxford, Lion Hudson, 2009.
3. Assuming that the speed of light has always been constant at 299,792 kilometers/second.
4. Davies, Paul, *God and the New Physics*, New York, Simon and Schuster, 1983.
5. Hawking, Stephen, *Black Holes and Baby Universes and Other Essays*, London, Bantam, 1993.
6. Poole, Michael, (Stannard, Russell ed.) *God for the 21st Century*, Radnor, Templeton, 2000.
7. Davies, Paul, *God and the New Physics*, New York, Simon and Schuster, 1983.
8. *The Universe: Past and Present Reflections*, article by Fred Hoyle in Engineering and Science, November, 1981.
9. Hawking, Stephen, *A Brief History of Time*, London, Bantam, 1988.
10. Bryson, Bill, *A Short History of Nearly Everything*, New York, Broadway, 2003.

[11] Gonzalez, Guillermo & Richards, Jay, *The Privileged Planet*, Regnery, Washington, 2006.

[12] *Lost in Migration: Earth's Magnetic Field Overdue a Flip*, article by Chris Wickham published on the Reuters News Agency website, October 3rd 2012.

[13] *Science Increasingly Makes the Case for God*, article by Eric Metaxas published in The Wall Street Journal, December 25th 2014. He goes on to say "Today there are more than 200 known parameters necessary for a planet to support life—every single one of which must be perfectly met, or the whole thing falls apart."

[14] Polkinghorne, John, *Quarks, Chaos and Christianity*, New York, Crossroad, 1994.

[15] Flew, Anthony, *There is a God: How the World's Most Notorious Atheist Changed His Mind*, New York, HarperCollins, 2007.

[16] *The Origin of Life on Earth*, article by Alonso Ricardo & Jack Szostak published on the Scientific American website, September 2009.

[17] Denton, Michael, *Evolution: A Theory in Crisis*, Bethesda, Adler and Adler, 1986.

[18] Lennox, John D., *God's Undertaker*, Oxford, Lion Hudson, 2009.

[19] Robertson, David, *The Dawkins Letters: Challenging Atheist Myths*, Fearn, Christian Focus, 2007.

[20] Bryson, Bill, *A Short History of Nearly Everything*, New York, Broadway, 2003.

[21] Dawkins, Richard, *River Out of Eden: A Darwinian View of Life* London, Phoenix, 1995.

[22] Quoted in Strobel, Lee, *The Case for a Creator*, Grand Rapids, Zondervan, 2004.

NOTES

[23] Humphreys, John, *In God We Doubt: Confessions of a Failed Atheist*, London, Hodder & Stoughton, 2007.

[24] Tate, Katherine, *My Father Bertrand Russell*, London, Victor Gollancz, 1976.

[25] Ortberg, John, *God Is Closer Than You Think*, Grand Rapids, Zondervan, 2005.

[26] Lewis, CS, *The Weight of Glory and Other Addresses*, London, SPCK, 1941.

[27] Lewis, CS, *Mere Christianity*, London, Collins, 1952.

[28] Templeton, John, *Possibilities for Over One Hundredfold More Spiritual Information: The Humble Approach in Theology and Science*, Templeton Foundation Press, 2000.

[29] Twain, Mark, *Following the Equator*, American Publishing Company, Hartford, 1897.

[30] Lewis, CS, *Mere Christianity*, London, Collins, 1952.

[31] Dawkins, Richard, *The God Delusion*, London, Bantam Press, 2006.

[32] Grudem, Wayne, *Systematic Theology*, Leicester, Inter-Varstiy Press, 1994.

[33] Lewis, CS, *Mere Christianity*, London, Collins, 1952.

[34] "And you will be hated by all for my name's sake. But the one who endures to the end will be saved (Mark 13.13) and "As it is, you do not belong to the world, but I have chosen you out of the world. That is why the world hates you." (John 15.19) for example.

[35] Muggeridge, Malcolm, *A Twentieth Century Testimony*, Nashville, Thomas Nelson, 1978.

[36] In a sermon on 1 Thessalonians 1.8-10 preached at Jesmond Parish Church, 12th April 1998, published on The Christian Institute's website.

[37] Stoner, Peter W., *Science Speaks, An Evaluation of Certain Christian Evidences*, Chicago, Moody Press 1957.

[38] Ayers, Martin, *Naked God: The Truth About God Exposed*, Epsom, Matthias Media, 2010.

[39] Stott, John, *The Contemporary Christian*, Leicester, Inter-Varsity Press, 1995.

[40] Wells, HG, *The Outline of History*, George Newnes, London, 1920.

[41] Phillips, Charles & Axelrod, Alan, *Encyclopedia of Wars*, New York, Facts on File, 2004.

[42] I have edited out the rhetorical repetition of the original. There are in fact several versions of the speech as it seemed he used the core of it on different occasions, adlibbing some of the detail.

[43] Oh, all right, if you've got your Greek Interlinear you can see it's technically *ho pollos*, the singular of *hoi polloi*.

[44] Mill, John Stuart, *Three Essays on Religion – Nature, the Utility of Religion and Theism*, London, Longmans, 1874.

[45] Farrar, Frederic W., *The Life of Christ*, New York, E.P. Dutton, 1891.

[46] Source: Dr. Ramsay MacMullen, History Professor Emeritus of Yale University, Dr. James Strange, Professor of Religious Studies, University of South Flordia, and Dr. Frederick Zugibe, Medical Examiner, in *How Jesus Died: The Final 18 Hours*, a documentary released by Trinity Pictures.

[47] Keller, Timothy, *The Reason for God: Belief in an Age of Skepticism*, New York, Penguin, 2008.

[48] Mark 3.20-21 and John 7.5, for example, show how hostile Jesus' brothers were to him during his three-year ministry.

[49] Ramsay, William Mitchell, *St. Paul the Traveller and the Roman Citizen*, London, Hodder & Stoughton, 1898.

[50] Morison, Frank, *Who Moved the Stone?*, London, Faber & Faber, 1930.

[51] See Mark 8.31-32, Mark 9.30-32 and Mark 10.32-34, where Jesus predicts his suffering, death and resurrection on three separate occasions.

[52] Lewis, CS, *God in the Dock*, Grand Rapids, Eerdmans, 1970.

[53] The genres I have in mind are legislation (e.g. Leviticus), historical narrative (e.g. 1 Kings), short story (e.g. Ruth), tragic poetry (e.g. Job), song lyrics (e.g. Psalms), tweets (e.g. Proverbs), romantic drama (Song of Solomon), prophecy (e.g. Isaiah), dirge poetry (e.g. Lamentations), news supplement (e.g. Mark), open letter (e.g. Ephesians), private correspondence (e.g. Philemon) and apocalyptic (e.g. Revelation).

[54] The Law of Moses prescribed the death penalty for cursing God, sacrificing to false gods, serious violations of the Sabbath, false prophecy, divination and the dabbling in various occult arts, human sacrifice, premeditated murder, kidnap, striking or cursing parents, persistent and incorrigible rebelliousness, rape, adultery, homosexual intercourse, incest, bestiality and premarital sex.

[55] John, J. and Walley, Chris, *The Life: a Portrait of Jesus*, Milton Keynes, Authentic, 2004.

[56] Pink AW, *The Divine Inspiration of the Bible*, Grand Rapids, Christian Classics Ethereal Library, 1917.

[57] *Bible In Norway Is Bestseller; 'The Scriptures' Surprisingly Strong In Largely Secular* Country, report by Saleha Mohsin published in The Huffington Post, June 6th 2013.

[58] Osowitt's full story is told on his church's website faithfellowshipnc.com, on the *Pastor Elliott's Testimony* page.

[59] Taylor, Richard with Miles, Richard, *To Catch a Thief: from Career Criminal to a Life of Hope*, Chichester, New Wine, 2006.

60. *Churches Stepping into Void in Recession Britain*, report by John Bingham published in The Daily Telegraph, February 5th 2013.

61. Knott, Geoff, *Church & Community Involvement; National Church Social Action Survey*, Research carried out by Jubilee Plus, December 2012.

62. *Local Church Full of Brainwashed Idiots Feeds Town's Poor Every Week*, report in The Onion, 3rd January 2014.

63. Quoted by Dilley, Andrea Palpant, *The Surprising Discovery about Those Colonialist, Proselytizing Missionaries*, article in Christianity Today, January-February 2014.

64. Piper, John, *Don't Waste Your Cancer*, Wheaton, Crossway, 2011.

65. Quoted in Zacharias, Ravi, *Has Christianity Failed You?*, Grand Rapids, Zondervan, 2010.

66. Guillebaud, Simon, *Dangerously Alive*, Oxford, Monarch, 2011.

67. Russell, Bertrand, *Autobiography*, London, George Allen & Unwin, 1975.

68. Wesley, John, *The Works of John Wesley Volume 1*, London, John Jones, 1809.

69. Piper, John, *A Godward Life by John Piper Savouring the Supremacy of God in All of Life*, Portland, Multnomah, 1997.

70. *Will South Korea become Christian?*, article by Christopher Landau, published on the BBC News website, October 26th 2009.

71. Press release for 2012 Church of England Finance Statistics, published 14 August 2014.

72. Chevreau, Guy, *Vital Signs of a Healthy Church: a Diagnostic*, Chichester, New Wine, 2008.

73. Moody, Raymond, *Life after Life*, San Francisco, HarperCollins, 1975.

74. www.iands.org/about-ndes.

[75] www.iands.org/about-ndes.

[76] Graham, Billy, *Death and the Life After*, Nashville, Thomas Nelson, 1987.

[77] *Eben Alexander, Harvard Neurosurgeon, Describes Heaven after Near-Death Experience*, report by Cavan Sieczkowski published in The Huffington Post, September 10th 2012.

[78] www.raymondmoody.org/transcendental-near-death-experience.

[79] Gaukroger, Stephen, *It Makes Sense*, London, Scripture Union, 1987.

[80] If you are troubled by or persuaded by the new atheists, I would like to recommend two YouTube films where Richard Dawkins and Christopher Hitchens debate with intelligent Christians on matters of faith. Google will take you to the right place if you type in *Lennox vs. Dawkins Debate - Has Science Buried God?* and *William Lane Craig vs. Christopher Hitchens Debate - Does God Exist?* These are not sound bite videos. They are quite long. The case for atheism, so engagingly made in the new atheist books, is given a rigorous critique and a proper run for its money. People will come to different conclusions about which argument comes out best. But certainly these debates expose the "Christians are deluded and brain-dead" narrative as the shameless propaganda it is.

[81] Dawkins, Richard, *The God Delusion*, London, Bantam Press, 2006.

[82] *As an Atheist, I Truly Believe Africa Needs God*, article by Matthew Parris, published in The Times, December 27th 2008.

[83] Czeslaw Milosz, *The Discrete Charm of Nihilism*, New York Review of Books, November 19th 1998.

[84] Spufford, Francis, *Unapologetic: Why, Despite Everything, Christianity Can Still Make Surprising Emotional Sense*, London, Faber & Faber, 2012.

[85] *Fox News' Highly Reluctant Jesus Follower*, article by Kirsten Powers, published in Christianity Today, November 2013.

[86] *Vicars Report Greatest Job Satisfaction While Publicans Are Least Happy*, article by Esther Addley, published in The Guardian, March 21st 2014.